Ronald Davies is a member of the St. Beuno's Outreach Team who introduce laymen and women to Ignatian Spirituality in the Diocese of Wrexham, North Wales.

Published by

MELROSE BOOKS

An Imprint of Melrose Press Limited
St Thomas Place, Ely
Cambridgeshire
CB7 4GG, UK
www.melrosebooks.com

EXPANDED SECOND EDITION

Copyright © Ronald S. Davies 2007, 2010

The Author asserts his moral right to
be identified as the author of this work

Cover designed by Tom Brennand

ISBN   978 1 907732 15 7

All rights reserved. No part of this publication may be reproduced,
stored in a retrieval system, or transmitted, in any form or by any means
electronic, mechanical , photocopying, recording or otherwise,
without the prior permission of the publishers.

This book is sold subject to the condition that it shall not,
by way of trade or otherwise, be lent, re-sold, hired out or
otherwise circulated without the publisher's prior consent
in any form of binding or cover other than that in which
it is published and without a similar condition including this
condition being imposed on the subsequent purchaser.

Printed and bound in Great Britain by:
CPI Antony Rowe, Chippenham, Wiltshire

Imaginative Contemplations

EXPANDED SECOND EDITION

by

Ronald S. Davies

I would like to dedicate this book to my good friend, the late John James Farrell.

Contents

		Page
Introduction		vii
1	Stilling Exercise	1
2	The Birth of John the Baptist Foretold - Luke 1: 5–25	3
3	The Annunciation – Luke 1: 26–38	9
4	The Visitation – Luke 1: 39–45	14
5	The Circumcision of John the Baptist - Luke 1: 59–66	18
6	The Nativity – Luke 2: 1–20	21
7	Jesus is Presented at the Temple - Luke 2: 22–38	26
8	Lectio Divina – Reading with God - John 1: 1–4	31
9	Jesus Among the Doctors of the Law – Luke 2: 41–50	34
10	The Baptism of Our Lord – Matthew 3: 13–17	40
11	The Temptation in the Wilderness – Luke 4: 1–13	44
12	The Wedding at Cana - John 2: 1–12	49
13	Jesus at Nazareth – Luke 4: 16–30	55
14:1	The First Four Disciples are Called – Mark 1: 16–20	62
14:2	The First Four Disciples are Called – Luke 5: 1–11	65
15	Jesus and the Pharisees - Luke 5: 27–39 and 6: 1–5	70
16	Cure of the Man with a Withered Hand – Luke 6: 6–11	76
17	The Call of Levi - Luke 6: 27–28	80
18	Cure of the Centurion's Servant - Luke 7: 1–10	83
19	The Woman who was a Sinner - Luke 7: 36–50	87
20	The Cure of Simon Peter's Mother-in-law – Mark 1: 29–31	93
21	Jesus Quietly Leaves Capernaum and Travels Through Galilee – Mark 1: 35–39	97
22	The Cure of the Paralytic – Mark 2: 1–12	102
23	Jesus Calms the Storm – Mark 4: 35–41	107
24	The Gerasene Demoniac – Mark 5: 1–20	111
25	Cure of a Blind Man at Bethsaida - Mark 8: 14–21	116
26	The Blind Man of Jericho - Mark 10: 46–52	121
27	Jesus and the Little Children - Mark 10: 13–16	125

28	Miracle of the Loaves – Luke 9: 12–17	128
29	Jesus Walks on Water and, With Him, Peter – Matthew 14: 22–33	132
30	The Adulterous Woman – John 8: 1–11	136
31	The Transfiguration – Luke 9: 28–36	141
32	The Epileptic Demoniac – Luke 9: 37–43	145
33	Who is the Greatest? - Luke 9: 46–48	149
34	Martha and Mary - Luke 10: 38–42	153
35	The Ten Lepers – Luke 17: 11–19	157
36	Zacchaeus – Luke 19: 1–10	162
37	The Resurrection of Lazarus - John 11: 1–44	168
38	The Anointing at Bethany - John 12: 1–11	176
39	The Messiah Enters Jerusalem - John 12: 12–19	181
40	Jesus Washes the Disciples' Feet – John 13: 1–5	185
41	The Eucharist – Matthew 26: 26–29	189
42	Gethsemane – Matthew 26: 36–46	192
43	The Arrest – Matthew 26: 47–56	197
44	Jesus Before Annas – John 18: 12–24	201
45	Peter's Denial – Luke 22: 54–62	205
46	Jesus Before the Sanhedrin – Mark 14: 55–65	209
47	Jesus Before Pilate – Luke 23: 2–7	213
48	Jesus Before Herod – Luke 23: 8–12	216
49	Jesus Before Pilate – John 18: 28–40	219
50	John 19: 1–11	225
51	Jesus Is Condemned to Death – John 19: 12–16	229
52	Jesus Carries His Cross – John 19: 17–18	231
53	The Crucifixion – Luke 23: 33–46	234
54	The Burial – Mark 15: 42–47	238
55	Lectio Divina – Reading with God – Psalm 130	242
56	The Empty Tomb – John 20: 1–10	245
57	Jesus Appears to Mary of Magdala – John 20: 11–18	248
58	The Road to Emmaus – Luke 24: 13–35	251
59	Jesus Appears to the Apostles – Luke 24: 35–48	256
60	Jesus at the Lakeside – John 21: 1–17	261
61	Pentecost – Acts 2: 1–13	266
62	Lectio Divina – Reading with God – John 14: 23–27	272
63	Three-way Conversation	275
64	Isaiah 55: 1–3	278
65	Isaiah 55: 6–9	280
66	The Sign of the Cross, Stilling	282

Introduction

'Imagination is the high road of faith.'

Cardinal Newman

The following Imaginative Contemplations can be used either in prayer groups or in private prayer.

Imaginative Contemplation is a way of praying recommended by St. Ignatius of Loyola and is used in his spiritual exercises.

The stilling exercise helps to calm the mind and can be used before you begin your chosen contemplation.

The contemplation should be read slowly, giving plenty of time to ponder each sentence or word.

By entering the chosen Gospel scene and imagining the reality of the story, even placing yourself in the scene, we come under the influence of the Holy Spirit which can enlighten our minds and console our spirit.

You are already a loved and forgiven child of God. You possess His Holy Spirit and all you need is His love and His grace.

1

Stilling Exercise

This stilling exercise is to help you to relax – before you begin your Imaginative Contemplation.

Sit as comfortably as you can, with a straight back.

Become aware of the room in which you have chosen to pray.

What sounds can you hear, outside and inside the room?

If you have lit a candle, focus on the flame or, in your mind's eye, picture the quiet, still flame. The golden flame, the black wick, the molten wax. Recall how you felt before you began to pray.

To still the mind you must first still the body.

Begin with your forehead. Relax any frowning or tension around the eyes.

Relax your cheek and jaw muscles.

Any tension in your neck and shoulders can be relaxed, let your shoulders fall, and let the weight of your arms pull your shoulders down.

Feel your arms relaxed, and become conscious of your hands resting quietly on your lap.

Now continue to be aware of your body. Focus on where your back presses against the chair.

Relax any tense muscles in your back and stomach.

Now focus on where the chair presses against your legs.

Just feel the weight of your body resting on the chair.

Now your legs, are they comfortable? Are the muscles in your thighs and calves relaxed?

Lastly your feet; feel the weight of them on the floor.

Become aware of your breathing; no need to change it, just be aware of the air entering and leaving your lungs.

You breathe in God's love, peace and forgiveness, breathe out your anxieties, negative thoughts and feelings.

You are His child, forgiven and loved.

He sends His Holy Spirit to help you to pray; you depend on Him and need His grace.

2

The Birth of John the Baptist Foretold - Luke 1: 5-25

In the days of King Herod of Judaea there lived a priest called Zechariah who belonged to the Abijah section of the priesthood, and he had a wife, Elizabeth by name, who was a descendant of Aaron. Both were worthy in the sight of God, and scrupulously observed all the commandments and observances of the Lord. But they were childless. Elizabeth was barren and they were both getting on in years.

Now it was the turn of Zechariah's section to serve, and he was exercising his priestly office before God when it fell to him by lot, as the ritual custom was, to enter the Lord's sanctuary and burn incense there. And at the hour of incense the whole congregation was outside, praying.

Then there appeared to him the angel of the Lord, standing on the right of the altar of incense. The sight disturbed Zechariah and he was overcome with fear. But the angel said to him, 'Zechariah, do not be afraid, your prayer has been heard. Your wife Elizabeth is to bear you a son and you must name him John. He will be your joy and delight and many will rejoice at his birth, for he will be great in the sight of the Lord. He must drink no wine, no strong drink. Even from his mother's womb he will be filled with the Holy Spirit, and he will bring back many of the sons of Israel to the Lord their God. With the spirit and power of Elijah, he will go before him to turn the hearts of the fathers towards their children and the disobedient back to the wisdom that the virtuous have, preparing for the Lord a people fit for him.' Zechariah said to the angel, 'How can I be sure of this? I am an old man and my wife is getting on in years.' The angel replied, 'I am Gabriel who stands in God's presence, and I have been sent to you and bring you this good news. Listen! Since you have not believed my words, which will come true at their appointed time, you will be silenced and have no power of speech until this has happened.' Meanwhile the people were waiting for Zechariah and were surprised that he stayed in the sanctuary so long. When he came out he could not speak to them, and they realised that he had received a vision in the sanctuary. But he could only make signs to them, and remained dumb.

When his time of service came to an end he returned home. Some time later his wife Elizabeth conceived and for five months she kept to herself. 'The Lord has done this for me,' she said, 'now that it has pleased him to take away the humiliation I suffered among men.'

❖❖❖

Can you see Zechariah standing by the incense altar?

An old man dressed in ceremonial robes.

Picture this sacred chamber, where only Priests can enter. By lottery Zechariah has been given the supreme honour of burning incense on the altar, an honour granted only once in a lifetime of Priestly service.

Oil lamps gild its walls of cedar, while dark corners hold their ancient mystery.

The Birth of John the Baptist Foretold - Luke 1: 5-25

The incense altar stands alone in a recess of the sanctuary with the lonely figure beside it.

He holds the golden incense boat ready but he seems distracted, deep in thought.

There is sadness in the eyes that gaze into the charcoal embers upon the altar.

A longing he thought long overcome now dominates his mind and the formal prayers cannot be found.

The chamber is silent with only the spluttering charcoal before his eyes.

He is thinking of the child he and his wife Elizabeth had longed for and all their prayers which had never been answered.

The painful longing has now returned with overpowering intensity and for no apparent reason.

Now at this sacred moment, in spite of his age he finds the deep longing for a child reawakened in his heart.

He is motionless and lost in thought, charcoal crackles in anticipation.

Voices outside become louder as psalms are sung and serve to remind Zechariah of his duties.

He throws incense on the glowing coals.

A thick cloud of blue smoke rises from the altar, the spluttering and spitting incense breaks the sanctuary's holy silence.

His reverie is broken, but still he cannot bring the customary prayers to mind.

The bubbling incense is now silent and its heavy perfume fills the air.

Blue smoke billows, and shapes form and fade above the altar.

Zechariah is now distracted by the strange movement around him.

The smoke has a life of its own and when it takes human shape, the incense spills from his hand and the amber crystals scatter at his feet.

His heart is racing as he falls to his knees in the presence of the unknown.

He is too afraid to look, and remains motionless with fear.

Nothing has prepared him for this, in spite of all his years of devoted service in the Temple.

A human voice calls his name and tells him not to be afraid because his prayer has been heard.

The voice is beautiful and calms him further by telling him his wife Elizabeth will conceive and bear a son who he must call John.

A gladness fills his whole being and Zechariah feels at peace, his fear has left him and he now looks at the Spirit of God, who brings such unexpected but wonderful news.

The mention of his wife's name and the actual name of his yet unborn son makes an unearthly experience very real.

The angel goes further not waiting for any response from Zechariah, 'He will be your joy and delight and many will rejoice at his birth, for he will be great in the sight of the Lord.'

Zechariah bows his head, this is all too much. Not just a child but a very special child will bless his marriage.

There is authority and a warning in the Spirit's voice as he tells him the child must not drink wine, or strong drink.

Zechariah is willing to accept any conditions and can only partially comprehend the Spirit when he also says, 'Even from his mother's womb your son will be filled with the Holy Spirit, and he will bring back many of the sons of Israel to the Lord their God. With the spirit and power of Elijah, he will go before him to turn the hearts of fathers towards their children and the disobedient back to the wisdom that the virtuous have, preparing for the Lord a people fit for him.'

Zechariah has said nothing. The sanctuary is silent. Smoke still swirls about the altar and envelops the two figures in the oil lamps' gentle light.

Zechariah feels the stiffness in his back and pain in his knees and he is reminded of his advanced years.

In a quiet voice he dares to speak and question the practicality of what he is hearing.

His maturity now enables him to look at the strange presence and ask, 'How can I be sure of this? I am an old man and my wife is getting on in years!'

The angel's voice is louder now and firmly tells him, 'I am Gabriel who stands in God's presence, and I have been sent to speak to you and bring you this good news.'

Zechariah feels admonished and bows his head, his questioning is unworthy.

'Listen,' says the angel. 'Since you have not believed my words, which will come true at the appointed time, you will be silenced and have no power of speech until this has happened.'

When he looks up his chastened eyes can see only the altar; the blue smoke has risen into the darkness of the ceiling. The angel has gone.

He still cannot move; he tries to recall all he heard the Angel say. He is honoured and yet humbled.

His joints are stiff and pain in his back and his knees slows his efforts to rise.

He replaces the incense boat on its shelf, still deep in thought, and then turning around he walks slowly out of the chamber.

He is met by anxious faces who want to know why he has been so long at prayer.

He had lost all sense of time and now he is speechless. How can he recount such an experience in simple words and which also concern his personal matters?

Zechariah's face glowing as if heated by a fire tells them that something exceptional has happened.

His efforts to convey his experience through gesture is futile and he remains silent, his thoughts still full of the angel's words and the Holy presence.

He leaves the Temple. Elizabeth should be the first to know what has happened.

3

The Annunciation – Luke 1: 26–38

In the sixth month the angel Gabriel was sent by God to a town in Galilee called Nazareth, to a virgin betrothed to a man named Joseph, of the House of David; and the virgin's name was Mary. He went in and said to her, 'Rejoice, you who enjoy God's favour! The Lord is with you.' She was deeply disturbed by these words and asked herself what this greeting could mean, but the angel said to her, 'Mary, do not be afraid; you have won God's favour. Look! You are to conceive in your womb and bear a son, and you must name him Jesus. He will be great and will be called the Son of the Most High. The Lord God will give him the throne of his ancestor David; he will rule over the house of Jacob for ever and his reign will have no end.' Mary said to the angel, 'But how can this come about, since I have no knowledge of man?' The angel answered, 'The Holy Spirit will come upon you, and the power of the Most High will cover you with its shadow. And so the child will be holy and will be called the Son of God. And I tell you this too: your cousin Elizabeth also, in her old age, has conceived a son, and she whom people called barren is now in her sixth month, for nothing is impossible to God.' Mary said, 'You see before you the Lord's servant, let it happen to me as you have said.' And the angel left her.

❖ ❖ ❖

Can you recall seeing pictures on television, pictures taken from space which show the earth in all its beauty?

Imagine God looking down on this planet, this planet which is our home.

There before him lies the Earth, suspended in space.

See the blackness of space, its incomprehensible infinity.

You can see millions of bright stars, all millions of light years away.

You can see the moon, the closest companion to the Earth; you can see clearly the many craters that scar its white surface.

Now you gaze with God at the beauty of the Earth.

See the vast blue oceans, the land masses of America, Africa, Asia, Europe.

What colours can you see? Green tropical forests, green fertile land, large cities and the yellow deserts of Africa, Asia and Australia.

There are the white snow caps in the north and south, the sun makes them shine.

Swirling cloud, white as angel's wings, embrace this perfect orb.

You are seeing what God could see when he decided the time had come to call his people back home, home where they really belong.

Look again with God as he surveys his beloved World, the people living their everyday lives, their worries and cares, their joys and sorrows. The sick, the suffering, the dying. The loving and hating. The conflicts. His people capable of destruction and creation. And always everywhere new birth.

The Annunciation – Luke 1: 26-38

So God gazes at his beloved creation, and his eyes rest on the part we call Europe, he searches the Mediterranean coast. He chooses to descend onto the East coast. See the land of Israel. Its sea shore, the green fertile land, bordered by desert.

He chooses an area called Galilee.

You can see many towns, shining white in the sun.

God is looking down on one town in particular, Nazareth. See the many flat roofed houses, climbing up the stony hills.

And God has chosen one of these houses, see its white clay brick walls, the steps leading to the flat roof.

Look now with him inside this home, what can you see?

An earth floor, washed clean, simple furniture, a bed covered with colourful blankets.

And there in this room sits a young girl, at her daily prayers.

What is she wearing? A simple dress, head covered modestly by a light veil.

The room is still, silent, peaceful.

What could Mary be praying? Reciting the well known Psalms, reading the scriptures that recount the many kings of Judea since David and before.

But today there are different thoughts entering her mind.

She feels a stirring in her heart.

These cannot be her thoughts. She feels God is telling her to listen, she must remain quiet.

She becomes alarmed, what is happening? She has never before felt his presence so strongly.

It's all so real she can see the angel of God before her, a beautiful figure full of light.

The angel tells her to remain calm and listen to what he has to say.

Her fears subside, she feels the benevolence of God; he can only bring good news; a sense of gladness is welling up inside her as the angel tells her that God has chosen her to be the mother of his beloved Son, whose name will be Jesus. The child she is to carry will follow in the steps of all the kings of the house of Jacob.

He will be the last king, and will be king forever.

She begins to feel greatly honoured, of great value, she has no fear.

The angel on bended knee before her looks into Mary's eyes. He waits for her response; so much depends on her reply. She gazes into the angel's eyes, they are still waiting for her to reply; patiently he waits, so much depends on her.

Mary's thoughts bring her some anxiety, how can this all be possible? She isn't married, the consequences could be disgrace, even death by stoning.

The angel sees her anxiety and tells her. There is no need to be afraid, God will protect her from all the danger and his Spirit which can do anything will plant the seed in her womb. 'Your child will be holy and the Son of God.'

Mary's deep faith and love for God now calms her mind; she feels full of gladness and hope for the future; all will be well.

She tells the waiting angel, 'I am the handmaid of the Lord, let what you have said be done unto me.'

The Annunciation – Luke 1: 26-38

The angel bows his head; God humbles himself before his own creation and shows her total respect.

The angel leaves her, her prayers are over. Now her daily tasks are to be all full of new purpose.

And now the angel that greeted Mary is kneeling before you, and is waiting. Can you accept the love God is offering you?

4

The Visitation – Luke 1: 39-45

Mary set out at that time and went as quickly as she could into the hill country to a town in Judah. She went into Zechariah's house and greeted Elizabeth. Now it happened that as soon as Elizabeth heard Mary's greeting, the child leapt in her womb and Elizabeth was filled with the Holy Spirit. She gave a loud cry and said, 'Of all the women you are the most blessed, and blessed is the fruit of your womb. Why should I be honoured with a visit from the mother of my Lord? Look, the moment your greeting reached my ears, the child in my womb leapt for joy. Yes, blessed is she who believed that the promise made her by the Lord would be fulfilled.'

❖❖❖

Can you imagine, in your mind's eye, a small village in the hills. The white stony hills of Judah.

The white houses are small, flat roofed, made of mud-bricks.

The streets are narrow; people stand in doorways; a man with a donkey is walking along the stony road; children are playing.

Put yourself on that street, hear the voices, the clatter of donkey's hooves on the cobbles; feel the warm sun on your face.

The Visitation – Luke 1: 39–45

As you watch the man with the donkey you can now see a man and a woman following behind. He seems a mature man, and the woman you can see is much younger.

Mary and Joseph are walking towards a house in this narrow, stony street.

They stop at a wooden door. See the wood, bleached by the sun; well worn around the latch by generations of people, the wood is dark and smoothed by many human hands.

Joseph knocks on the door; hear the sound as his knuckles strike the wood.

The door opens; a middle-aged woman stands in the doorway; you can see that she is pregnant.

When she sees Mary she immediately throws up her arms, and with a great cry of delight she embraces Mary; a joyful greeting.

The three of them now enter the small, dark house.

The floor has been washed; the room is cool.

The bed against the wall is covered with folded colourful blankets.

An older man, Zechariah, is seated at the table; he doesn't speak.

Mary, Joseph and Elizabeth go and sit with him.

Elizabeth takes hold of Mary's hand and, with tears in her eyes, tells her how wonderful it is to see her. She looks deeply into Mary's eyes and tells her that her baby leapt in her womb when she saw Mary and she had been filled with joy.

Before Mary arrived she had been so happy and glad she was to become a mother after all these years but now she understood what her husband had been trying to tell her. That the child was to do great things for God.

And now Mary was also to give birth to a wonderful child.

Joseph listens to Mary as she tells Elizabeth about her own experiences.

He has questioned what she had told him. Was she really pregnant? How could she be?

He had heard of Zechariah's experience in the temple, how he had been profoundly moved by the revelation and promises made to him about his own child.

Joseph could only accept the truth and the genuine wonder and humility expressed by these three people.

This visit has been a turning point in his life.

All his doubts have disappeared.

The woman he loves is involved in something bigger than anything they could have imagined or that they can fully comprehend.

They become silent; a stillness fills the room.

The sunlight slants through the window as they try to understand all that has been happening to them.

In a quiet voice you hear Mary say, 'My heart is full of gladness; my spirit has never known such joy, to know that the Almighty has condescended to bestow on me such a privilege and honour.'

Joseph knows now he has a part to play.

Mary, he understands, needs his full support and protection. He is the only one who can save her reputation and make the birth of her baby possible.

The Visitation – Luke 1: 39–45

He suggests that Mary should stay until Elizabeth gives birth to her son.

Watch now as Joseph takes his leave. He embraces Zechariah, then Elizabeth and finally his beloved Mary.

He leaves through the door he entered and steps into the sunny street. You too can feel the sun on your face, hear the children.

Watch as he walks away, happy to prepare a place for Mary and himself to live and where Mary can give birth to her son.

Lord, may we have some share in the joy and gladness of Mary, Elizabeth, Zechariah and Joseph. Help us be aware of Your presence in our everyday lives, so that whatever we do, it will be to Your greater honour and glory. Amen.

In your prayer time, recall the thoughts and feelings you experienced during your prayer.

5

The Circumcision of John the Baptist – Luke 1: 59–66

Now on the eighth day they came to circumcise the child: they were going to call him Zechariah after his father, but his mother spoke up. 'No,' she said, 'he is to be called John.' They said to her, 'But no one in your family has that name' and made signs to his father to find out what he wanted him called. The father asked for a writing tablet and wrote, 'His name is John.' And they were all astonished. At that instant his power of speech returned and he spoke and praised God. All their neighbours were filled with awe and the whole affair was talked about throughout the hill country of Judaea. All those who heard of it treasured it in their hearts. 'What will this child turn out to be?' they wondered. And indeed the hand of the Lord was with him.

❖❖❖

The long fruitless marriage of Zechariah and Elizabeth has been transformed by the birth of a son.

In their old age they gaze in wonder and love at the new life which has entered their remaining years.

The Circumcision of John the Baptist - Luke 1: 59-66

Their childless marriage and devotion to God has now been fulfilled. They are true servants of God and he has shown them his redeeming power.

Zechariah still cannot speak about his intimate experience with God in the Sanctuary.

He can only look at the child in his mother's arms with wonder and gratitude; his deepest longing has been satisfied and he is more than content.

The child is now eight days old and the house is full of family, friends and neighbours who have come to witness and celebrate his circumcision.

The child will be named today and they are congratulating Zechariah who now has an heir who will keep his name in the Priestly line.

The Priest takes the knife in preparation, but Elizabeth interrupts the animated onlookers and shocks everyone by saying in a firm voice that the child's name will be John and not Zechariah.

There is silence, the Priest stands surprised by this unexpected outburst from Elizabeth and the break in family tradition.

They all turn to Zechariah, who has been silent during the whole pregnancy, and they mistakenly try to communicate with him through gestures.

Why is he so passive? Surely he is not going to allow this to happen, he must use his authority.

Zechariah sees their questioning faces and rising from his chair he points to the much used writing tablet which is given to him.

He writes with a slow, deliberate hand, 'His name is John.'

The tablet is passed around the room.

In amazement they all turn again to Elizabeth, expecting some explanation.

Are the parents disowning the child? There is a composed detachment in the parents, which is hard to understand.

Their child is a gift from God and they are the loving guardians.

Zechariah is a changed man; no longer hidden and silent he now stands near the mother and child and, his heart filled with joy, he can speak at last, his strong voice sings out a loud proclamation.

'Blessed be the Lord, the God of Israel for he has visited his people, he has come to their rescue and he has raised up for us a power of salvation in the House of his servant David, even as he proclaimed, by the mouth of his holy prophets from ancient times, that he would save us from our enemies and from the hands of all who hate us. Thus he shows his mercy to our ancestors, thus he remembers his holy covenant, the oath he swore to our father Abraham that he would grant us, free from fear, to be delivered from the hands of our enemies, to serve him in holiness and virtue in his presence, all our days. And you, little child, you shall be called Prophet of the Most High, for you will go before the Lord to prepare the way for him. To give his people knowledge of salvation through the forgiveness of their sins; this by the tender mercy of our God who from on high will bring the rising Sun to visit us, to give light to those who live in darkness and the shadow of death, and to guide our feet into the way of peace.'

6

The Nativity – Luke 2: 1–20

Now it had happened that at this time Caesar Augustus issued a decree that a census should be made of the whole inhabited world. This census – the first – took place while Quirinius was Governor of Syria, and everyone went to be registered, each to his own town. So Joseph set out from the town of Nazareth in Galilee for Judaea, to David's town called Bethlehem, since he was of David's House and line, in order to be registered together with Mary, his betrothed, who was with child. Now it happened that, while they were there, the time came for her to have her child, and she gave birth to a son, her firstborn. She wrapped him in swaddling clothes and laid him in a manger because there was no room for them in the living-space. In the countryside close by there were shepherds out in the fields keeping guard over their sheep during the watches of the night. An angel of the Lord stood over them and the glory of the Lord shone round them. They were terrified, but the angel said, 'Do not be afraid. Look, I bring you news of great joy, a joy to be shared by the whole people. Today in the town of David a Saviour has been born to you; he is Christ the Lord. And here is a sign for you: you will find a baby wrapped in swaddling clothes and lying in a manger.' And all at once with the angel there was a great throng of the hosts of heaven, praising God with the words: 'Glory to God in the highest heaven, and on Earth, peace for those he favours.'

Now it happened that when the angels had gone from them into heaven, the shepherds said to one another, 'Let us go to Bethlehem and see this event which the Lord has made known to us.' So they hurried away and found Mary and Joseph, and the baby lying in the manger. When they saw the child they repeated what they had been told about him, and everyone who heard it was astonished at what the shepherds said to them. As for Mary, she treasured all these things and pondered them in her heart. And the shepherds went back glorifying and praising God for all they had heard and seen, just as they had been told.

❖❖❖

Imagine a dark, still night over the hills near Bethlehem.

There are many hills in Israel; all have commanding views which lead onwards to further hills.

All are dry and rocky; sparse grass struggles to grow in the dry soil. Juniper bushes, gorse and yellow broom give it colour.

But tonight all this is hidden in darkness. The sky with its millions of stars dominates the world.

Now, see among the rocks three shepherds, all sitting near a small fire.

See their faces lit by the warm flames.

The sheep they care for are feeding on the hill; they know better than to wander far from the firelight and the men.

The night is still and quiet; all three sit in silence and gaze in wonder at the stars that cover the sky from one horizon to the other, a great dome that tonight seems near enough to touch.

The Nativity – Luke 2: 1–20

These simple men can't help wondering at the majesty of the universe in which they live.

They might know that they are social outcasts, have no place in society; the lowest of ranks, they have no vote nor can they witness in a court of law.

Tonight they feel the richest men on Earth; they are part of God's magnificent creation. They feel small but honoured and bless Jahweh for His majesty.

And so they gaze silently together, glad of each other's company, but strangely aware tonight of the immensity of God's creation.

Their eyes become fixed on a bright star they had not noticed before; together as they look it becomes bigger and bigger until the light from it makes the rest of the heavens disappear.

The hill is lit by a pure light brighter than anything they had ever seen. The light floods all the surrounding hills.

In the light they can see movement; figures seem to be welcoming and praising a divine spirit, God Himself, the Almighty Jehovah, Creator of the universe. The figures have their backs to the shepherds and in adoration face upwards into the light; the shepherds cannot see what the angels see, but they share in their profound reverence and love. Whatever is descending is of great value and adored.

A figure now leaves the host and approaches the shepherds.

The light and joyful singing increases and the shepherds begin to feel afraid.

The angel tells them not to fear, they must just listen.

The air becomes still, the pure light engulfs them and they feel part of this rejoicing throng of angels.

The angel tells them, 'I bring you news of great joy, a joy to be shared by the whole people. Today in the town of David a Saviour has been born to you; he is Christ the Lord. And here is a sign for you: you will find a baby wrapped in swaddling clothes and lying in a manger.'

The shepherds feel that they and the whole world are being given something of unimaginable value; they share the gladness of the angel even though they cannot fully understand.

And now there seem to be even more angels singing; the beautiful music and the pure white light increase, all confirming what the angel said.

The last thing the shepherds hear is a great shout in the heavens that echoes in the hills, 'Glory to God in the highest heavens and peace to men who enjoy God's favour,' and the light begins to fade and grows dim until the stars appear again in the dark sky above and silence returns to the hilltop.

The shepherds don't speak. They look down onto Bethlehem below; they feel changed; they feel energised; they feel compelled to do what the angel told them to do.

One is chosen to stay with the sheep while the others set off down the hillside.

As they get near to Bethlehem, the town still sleeps; the only light comes from a stable next to an inn.

As they approach they hear voices and the cry of a newborn baby.

They look in over the stable door.

Candles and oil lamps light the scene.

A young girl has just finished wrapping her baby in swaddling clothes and is placing the child in the clean straw of a manger.

There is an older man, his arm around the girl's shoulders, looking fondly and with wonder at his new son.

Women who helped with the birth are clearing away the afterbirth and blood-stained clothing.

The shepherds enter the stable; they approach Mary and Joseph and they look in awe at the baby.

Will anyone believe what they have to say?

They can't help themselves; they look into Mary's eyes and tell her with breathless wonder what they have experienced on the hill.

Mary is not alarmed; she receives the news calmly. It's as if this is expected, not a surprise but a confirmation; she too has felt the presence of the angel, and she looks with even greater wonder at her newborn son.

Mary and Joseph thank the shepherds who now gaze in wonder at the child; this child has been the cause of rejoicing and gladness which they had shared with the angels on the hilltop.

This child is of tremendous value and deeply loved by Jahweh, and now he is dependent on you, how will the world receive him?

You also are close to the manger and Mary gently lifts the baby and places him in your arms.

Look at the child in your arms, his tiny hands and feet, the short hair on his head and that old wrinkled look of a newborn baby.

7

Jesus is Presented at the Temple - Luke 2: 22-38

And when the day came for them to be purified as laid down by the Law of Moses, they took him up to Jerusalem to present him to the Lord – observing what stands written in the Law of the Lord: Every first born male must be consecrated to the Lord – and also to offer in sacrifice, in accordance with what is said in the Law of the Lord, a pair of turtle doves or two young pigeons. Now in Jerusalem there was a man named Simeon. He was an upright and devout man; he looked forward to Israel's comforting and the Holy Spirit rested on him. It had been revealed to him by the Holy Spirit that he would not see death until he had set eyes on the Christ of the Lord. Prompted by the Spirit he came to the Temple: and when the parents brought in the child Jesus to do for him what the Law required, he took him into his arms and blessed God; and he said: 'Now, Master, you can let your servant go in peace, just as you promised; because my eyes have seen the salvation which you have prepared for all the nations to see, a light to enlighten the pagans and the glory of your people Israel.'

As the child's father and mother stood there wondering at the things that were being said about him, Simeon blessed them and said to Mary his mother, 'You see this child; he is destined for the fall and for the rising of many in Israel, destined to be a sign that is rejected – and a sword will pierce your own soul too – so that the secret thoughts of many may be laid bare.'

Jesus is Presented at the Temple - Luke 2: 22-38

There was a prophetess also, the daughter of Phanuel, of the tribe of Asher. She was well on in years. Her days of childhood over, she had been married for seven years before becoming a widow. She was now eighty-four years old and never left the Temple, serving God night and day with fasting and prayer. She came by just at that moment and began to praise God; and she spoke of the child to all who looked forward to the deliverance of Jerusalem.

❖❖❖

Mary sits with her precious child and sings softly of the old kings of Israel.

With the warmth of her body the baby sleeps in her arms.

The love in her heart for her child extends to the giver of all her joy.

She remembers her duty as a mother and in acknowledgement of her great gift she must approach the giver and show her gratitude and respect.

Her eyes wander from the baby's sleeping face and rest on Joseph working at his carpenter's bench; the man who supported her through the dangerous period following her consent to conceive a child before marriage.

She rises holding the baby and speaks to Joseph who lays down his tools, and agrees that the time has come to present their child in the Temple.

The chosen day has arrived. The faithful donkey is prepared for Mary and the baby, the carpenter's shop is shut securely and the family take the familiar road from Nazareth to Jerusalem.

Hear the donkey's hooves now on the cobbled street; Joseph, staff in hand leads the way out of the town into the country. Can you feel as they do, the breeze on your face and the warm sun on your back, hear the clatter of startled birds in the trees?

They adore their child, the most precious thing in their lives, but they also know that Yahweh loves him even more and it is with this rapturous feeling of being part of the loving family of God that they now look forward to showing their respect and love for the loving Spirit of God.

What the future holds is not known, but now is the time for gladness as the family reach Jerusalem.

They enter the massive gates of the Temple; the busy courtyard is crowded with market stalls and pilgrims. Hear the traders cries, the crash and rattle of coins in the money changers' bags, the soft cooing of doves.

See the wild pigeons fly from the lofty walls and strut among the buyers feet pecking at the ground for fallen grain.

Joseph ties the donkey securely and pays a boy to mind him while he and Mary go to the stall selling small birds for sacrifice.

They buy two turtle doves, all that they can afford.

They now enter the chamber where every first born male is consecrated to God and where Mary will be purified.

Mary now uncovers the child and at once a man moves towards her. He is not a Temple official but from his appearance she can tell he is a respectable man.

Joseph watches as the man stands looking at the baby, his face radiant, his eyes full of tears and his hands raised in wonder.

Jesus is Presented at the Temple - Luke 2: 22-38

Mary is not afraid and Joseph allows the stranger to hold the baby in his arms, and is surprised at his immediate trust in the man.

He tells them his name is Simeon and with a radiant smile he explains that all his life he has looked forward to the comforting of Israel and that the Spirit of God has revealed to him that before he dies he will see the anointed one of God.

Today the Spirit has made him come to the Temple and now his joy is unbounded.

He is glad, glad beyond measure, his life of devotion has been fulfilled and with the baby in his arms he raises his face to the sky and says, 'Now Master you can let your servant go in peace, just as you promised; because my eyes have seen the salvation which you have prepared for all the nations to see; a light to lighten the pagans and the glory of your people Israel.'

Mary and Joseph listen, their own faith is also confirmed by his words; the Spirit he speaks of has also transformed their lives and they can share an intimacy with Simeon which will strengthen them in the years to come.

Simeon, the tears brimming over, gently hands the child back to his mother.

Powerful emotions have drained Simeon and Joseph now sees a venerable old man before him who now gives them his blessing but also gives them a warning, and to Mary he says, 'You see this child; he is destined for the fall and for the rising of many in Israel, destined to be a sign that is rejected – and a sword will pierce your own soul too so that the secret thoughts of many may be laid bare.'

Mary's happiness is diminished by his words but she is willing to accept anything that pleases God, she is still his handmaid.

They are taking their leave and turn to go. An old woman often seen in the Temple has been listening to Simeon and now she too expresses her joy in seeing the baby. She wants to tell the world the good news that deliverance from all evil is now at hand.

The family's visit to the Temple has been a milestone in their lives. The mystery surrounding the child's birth is deepening.

Even so life must go on, and they return to Nazareth the way they came, Joseph to his work and Mary to her work as wife and mother.

Psalm 100

Acclaim Yahweh, all the earth,
serve Yahweh gladly
come into his presence with songs of joy!
Know that he, Yahweh is God,
He made us and we belong to him,
we are his people, the flock that he pastures.
Walk through his porticos giving thanks
enter his courts praising him,
give thanks to him, bless his name.
Yes Yahweh is good,
his love is everlasting,
his faithfulness endures from age to age.

8

Lectio Divina – Reading with God

John 1: 1–4

Something which has existed since the beginning, which we have heard, which we have seen with our own eyes, which we have watched and touched with our own hands, the Word of life – this is our theme. That life was made visible, we saw it and are giving our testimony, declaring to you the eternal life, which was present to the Father and has been revealed to us. We are declaring to you what we have seen and heard, so that you too may share our life. Our life is shared with the Father and with his Son, Jesus Christ. We are writing this to you so that our joy may be complete.

❖ ❖ ❖

Something, something that existed, was alive before the universe or time was created.

Something – do we give it a name? Was it love, was it light, was it truth, life itself?

Was this something benevolent?

It created us – would we hate something which we had created? More likely we would love, cherish and protect it.

Something created us, wanted us to exist.

Wanted us to be part of His created universe.

We have heard the voice of this Creator, heard with our own ears. What we are telling you is not hearsay.

We have seen him with our own eyes.

We watched him as he preached, watched him heal the sick.

We watched him pray, we celebrated with him and we watched him suffer.

We have been close to him. Felt his hands wash our feet, his hand upon our shoulder encouraging us to have faith and be at peace because his Father loves us.

God spoke; His word, the word He spoke, gave us our lives. Life itself became visible to us; it became flesh and blood like us.

Yes, we saw Him, shared three years of His life on Earth as a man.

And this is our testimony, telling you of the eternity which belongs to us all.

The eternity which belongs to the Father was made visible to us.

What we have seen and heard is the truth and not second-hand.

We are telling you all this so that you can join us, and become part of God's family again.

We apostles have become part of God's family and now we share His love for you.

Our happiness cannot be complete until you also are in God's family again, united with this something that created us, and united through His beloved Son. Something which has existed since time began, wants us to be with Him forever.

9

Jesus Among the Doctors of the Law

~ Luke 2: 41–50

Every year his parents used to go to Jerusalem for the feast of the Passover. When he was twelve years old, they went up for the feast as usual. When they were on their way home after the feast, the boy Jesus stayed behind in Jerusalem without his parents knowing it. They assumed he was with the caravan, and it was only after a day's journey that they went to look for him among their relations and acquaintances. When they failed to find him they went back to Jerusalem looking for him everywhere.

Three days later, they found him in the Temple, sitting among the doctors, listening to them and asking them questions; and all those who heard him were astounded at his intelligence and replies. They were overcome when they saw him, and his mother said to him, 'My child, why have you done this to us? See how worried your father and I have been, looking for you.' 'Why were you looking for me?' he replied. 'Did you not know that I must be busy with my Father's affairs?' But they did not understand what he meant.

❖ ❖ ❖

Jesus Among the Doctors of the Law – Luke 2: 41-50

Imagine you have been the father of Jesus for twelve years. He has been an obedient child and readily learned the trade of a carpenter under your direction.

He has taken pride in his work and respects you and his mother Mary. He is close to his mother; they share a special bond which you accept even though you don't understand.

You have never felt excluded; the boy's respect and love for you is sincere.

Jesus knows how to work hard but he also enjoys the company of his peers. He has been free to play as a child with other children in Nazareth, and now as he approaches manhood he mixes with older boys sharing experiences of growing up.

His twelfth year has arrived, the age when Jewish boys become men.

This year the visit to Jerusalem to celebrate the feast of the Passover is going to be special: Jesus will return home as a man, a boy no longer.

The family look forward to the event and you have made arrangements with the neighbours to travel together to Jerusalem.

Some of Jesus' friends are of the same age as himself and will all share in the feast of the Passover.

You and Mary have packed all you need and loaded it onto the donkey's back. This old donkey is still able to serve you as he did on the journey to Bethlehem.

Now you have another donkey which Mary can ride.

Your son Jesus walks along with you on the dry stony road that leads to Jerusalem. You are familiar with the route and know that it will take a full day's journey to get there.

You now arrive at Jerusalem. The place always impresses you: its great protective walls and towers, the magnificent temple that dominates the city.

You make your way to the familiar camping ground in the Kidron Valley. This is a good place, near the golden gate close to the Temple.

There are food stalls set up where you can buy all you need and you set up the tent where Mary has chosen to be close to your friends and near a stream where you can wash.

When all is finished you let Jesus go exploring with his friends. There is much to see.

People have arrived from other parts of Israel. Some dress differently according to their region, some have camels heavily decorated with tassels and beads. Fringes hang over their long faces, dark eyes shine behind them.

Jesus has an outgoing nature and shows great interest in the many strangers now in Jerusalem.

The next day after an evening spent with your friends, it's time to visit the temple where you will celebrate the Passover.

You take Jesus into the Temple. He is old enough now to appreciate the great significance of all that surrounds him.

He sees the families taking their sacrifices to the priests. The priests' awesome presence as they address the people. He sees their elaborate clothes, and the sanctity of the forbidden Holy of Holies, that mysterious place where man meets God.

Jesus, your son, has recited from the scriptures and has been accepted by the elders as a man in his own right and you are proud of him.

Jesus Among the Doctors of the Law – Luke 2: 41-50

The Passover is finished. Your visit to Jerusalem has been successful and special, and now is the time to leave.

You and Mary on the second morning of your stay begin to pack your belongings onto the donkey. Mary has bought some material to take home and you some tools which can only be bought in Jerusalem.

And so you set off. The boys are all together, still sharing the pleasure of having manly status.

Anxious to get back home to work, you and Mary leave the camping site and with your neighbours you make a long trail of people and animals forming a small caravan of travellers.

All day you journey and eventually arrive home in Nazareth, hot and tired.

Why isn't Jesus here to help unload? His friends have gone to their homes, where is he?

You search but cannot find him. His friends say they haven't seen him since they were in Jerusalem.

Your heart is suddenly gripped with cold dread. Immediately you and Mary are leaving Nazareth and mounted on the donkeys you ride in great haste back along the road to Jerusalem. It will take all night and you will arrive soon after dawn.

Your feelings are mixed. There is dread, great anguish but also anger – how could he be so disobedient? But concern for the son you love makes undesirable thoughts haunt your imagination. What has happened to him?

You arrive again at the camping ground. It's empty; no young boy stands anxiously waiting for your return.

Where can he be? Where do you start your search? You ask the tradesmen still at their stalls, but they are no help. You have searched for three days. It's now nearly five days since you realised he was missing. It's time to think.

You remember how impressed he had been with everything he had seen in the Temple and had spent many hours wandering about its courts.

He must still be there, lost in its endless corridors. Your pulse quickens. You take Mary by the hand and enter the Temple.

The size of the building is daunting. Crowds of people fill the courtyards.

You see some youths of Jesus' age leave one of the schools where the doctors hold seminars.

You hear voices coming from the building and you stand at the open door and look at the scene before you.

Against the far wall are seated many doctors of law and scripture, all conversing with a group of youths who are sitting at their feet.

Your heart fills with relief and joy as you recognise the head of your son as he sits gazing up at the elders.

You embrace Mary as you direct her searching eyes towards Jesus who she immediately recognises.

You cannot disrupt the scene. Any anger has left you and is replaced by wonder and some pride to see your son conversing with ease with the elders who seem pleased to answer his questions and even show surprise and interest in his comments concerning the scriptures and the prophets.

You can see a change in him: he looks and sounds grown up. He converses with the elders on equal terms, not as a pupil. He looks so much at home and is oblivious to you and his mother, unaware of time and place. This is where he belongs.

Nonetheless he cannot stay: the Passover has finished days ago and there is work to be done at home. He cannot stay with these seminarians, it's not practical. Never have you thought of him becoming a priest or rabbi.

You quietly approach Jesus and tap him gently on the shoulder. He looks up. The surprise on his face shows his complete lack of any awareness of the anguish he has caused.

He responds at once and after bowing to the elders he leaves the building with you and Mary.

His mother is relieved and like any anxious mother she hugs him, but also remonstrates with him, 'My child, why have you done this to us? See how worried your father and I have been, looking for you.'

You see in your son's face the innocence of someone who sincerely can see nothing wrong in their behaviour. 'Why were you looking for me? Did you not know that I must be busy with my Father's affairs?'

You and Mary can understand to a certain degree. You have never forgotten his birth in Bethlehem and the prophecies concerning him. You must allow him freedom to fulfil his destiny.

Your son has changed more than you expected. He has found his true home and his whole being has been caught up in his search for God who he calls Father.

But you cannot afford to pay for his education in the temple; he must return home and continue to earn a living as a carpenter.

With remarkable detachment the boy willingly leaves the temple with you and his mother. Your journey home is joyful and sad. Your son is no longer a child but a man with a life of his own.

10

The Baptism of Our Lord –

Matthew 3: 13–17

Then Jesus appeared. He came from Galilee to the Jordan to be baptised by John. John tried to dissuade him, with the words, 'It is I who need baptism from you, and yet you come to me!' But Jesus replied, 'Leave it like this for the time being; it is fitting that we should, in this way, do all that uprightness demands.' Then John gave in to him.

And when Jesus had been baptised he at once came up from the water, and suddenly the heavens opened and he saw the Spirit of God descending like a dove and coming down on him. And suddenly there was a voice from heaven, 'This is my Son, the Beloved; my favour rests on him.'

❖❖❖

Picture the scene before you.

You are sitting on a river bank.

The water is clear and shallow.

The Baptism of Our Lord – Matthew 3: 13–17

You can see the small pebbles on the river bed.

Small fish are darting among the stones and green weed.

The grass beneath you is short; feel its coolness with your hand.

Feel the sun on your face, a gentle breeze in your hair.

A beautiful sunny day; white clouds glide across the blue sky.

The sun glints on the gently flowing river; hear the sound it makes.

In the river you can see a man standing waist-deep.

A wild-looking man, with unkempt hair and beard, dressed in animal skins; a strange, lonely man from the desert.

You are not alone on the river bank.

Jesus is sitting on the grass next to you.

You are feeling strangely relaxed in his company. There is no need to speak.

The silence between you is comforting.

The sun is warming you and him.

Without speaking, Jesus slowly removes his sandals.

His thoughts have led him to a decision.

You watch as he stands up and walks the short distance over the grass and into the river.

His feet are now in the clear water.

He walks further until he is now waist deep and close to the man you observed before.

Jesus humbly asks John to baptise him.

John seems reluctant at first but Jesus persuades him, and you watch as Jesus is immersed in the clean, cool water.

You now see Jesus standing in the river, water streaming from his hair, over his shoulders and down his body.

The sun glints on his wet hair; a brightness seems to envelop him. In this light a pure white bird is hovering above Jesus' head.

Mixed with the gentle, rippling sound of water you hear a voice saying, 'This is my Son, my beloved Son, in whom I am well pleased; my favour rests on him.'

You now watch as Jesus walks out of the river and comes back to sit with you again.

Jesus turns to you and says, 'Now it's your turn.'

He encourages you to stand up and walk down the bank.

Feel the cool grass under your feet.

The shallow water and the smooth pebbles.

The clear water gets deeper until it's up to your waist, and you are standing next to John.

He gently holds you as you are lowered into the water.

Your face is under the water. You can see the sun and blue sky through the water.

You are helped to stand up again. John is holding your shoulders as the water runs down from your head.

The sunlight is dazzling, flashing off the water; the river ripples around you and you hear, deep in your heart, the voice again saying, 'You are my beloved son, my beloved daughter. I am very pleased with you.' Hear God call your name; he knows you better than you know yourself.

The Baptism of Our Lord – Matthew 3: 13–17   43

You feel greatly consoled as you walk through the water back to your place on the bank beside Jesus.

Feel again the smooth stones, the short grass.

You sit next to Jesus, your brother. The sun now warms you both as you sit in silence together.

Psalm 52

I for my part, like an olive tree
Growing in the house of God
Put my trust in God's love
For ever and ever.

I mean to thank You constantly
For doing what You did
And put my hope in Your name,
That is so full of kindness,
In the presence of those who love You.

Prayer

God, our Father, open my eyes to discover the vision that You have for me. Lead me to grow in faith and confidence that You have truly made me in Your own image and likeness, and You call me by my name. As with Your beloved Son Jesus, You say to me, 'You are my well-beloved son/daughter, and my favour rests on you.'

11

The Temptation in the Wilderness

~ Luke 4: 1-13

Filled with the Holy Spirit, Jesus left the Jordan and was led by the Spirit into the desert, for forty days being put to the test by the devil. During that time he ate nothing and at the end he was hungry. Then the devil said to him, 'If you are the Son of God, tell the stone to turn into a loaf.' But Jesus replied, 'Scripture says: "Human beings live not on bread alone."'

Then, leading him to a height, the devil showed him in a moment of time all the kingdoms of the world and said to him, 'I will give you all this power and their splendour, for it has been handed over to me, for me to give it to anyone I choose. Do homage, then, to me, and it shall all be yours.' But Jesus answered him, 'Scripture says: "You must do homage to the Lord your God; Him alone you must serve."'

Then he led him to Jerusalem and set him on the parapet of the temple. 'If you are the Son of God,' he said to him, 'Throw yourself down from here, for scripture says: "He has given his angels orders about you, to guard you," and again: "They will carry you in their arms in case you trip over a stone."'

But Jesus answered him, 'Scripture says: "Do not put the Lord your God to the test."'

Having exhausted every way of putting him to the test, the devil left him, until the opportune moment.

❖❖❖

Jesus has been baptised by John in the River Jordan.

Jesus has identified himself with humanity; even though he was sinless he had been cleansed by water.

Picture him standing on the riverbank, his thoughts still full of the words he heard from his Father: 'You are my beloved Son.'

His Father had encouraged and consoled him, confirmed his identity not only to Jesus but to all those being baptised that day.

These are powerful, overwhelming thoughts.

Jesus feels he has a lot to think about.

He needs time and space in which to think and pray. He needs to find the way forward.

To discover what his Father really wants from him.

Watch as Jesus quietly leaves the people by the river and makes his way up the hillside.

The ground he walks on is dry and stony; a few dry shrubs and rocks.

You can see him now on the high ground.

The sun is hot; no shelter.

Jesus pulls his hood over his head, partly to protect himself from the heat, and partly to help him think.

You now see him days later, far into the silent, lonely desert. Wind is stirring the sand; lizards scurry about.

Like the tribes of Israel he has been in the desert; they for forty years, himself forty days.

They had been tempted and failed.

He was to be severely tempted as well.

The humanity of Jesus was leading his thoughts away from God.

Like anyone else would be, he was hungry and thirsty.

The devil in him suggested he used his divine powers to provide all his physical needs by turning the stones into bread.

He could do anything; he had the power to change any circumstance to his advantage. People would flock to him for all their material needs. He would be a successful Messiah.

But no, there is more to life than material needs and prosperity.

His mind relaxes; he leaves those thoughts behind.

But now another thought enters his mind. He moves to a different place. In his mind's eye he sees all the kingdoms on Earth. The splendour, glory and power these kingdoms have. With his divine power he could rally men to arms and overcome these kingdoms, and by the sword bring all these people to God. With God's power, he could take the Roman Empire.

But no! Force, violence, suppression would not be his Father's way.

God's way was to be the only way; whatever that was to be, it was not to be one of domination and slavery.

Jesus' mind is at peace again and he thanks his Father.

The Temptation in the Wilderness – Luke 4: 1–13

But now another thought enters his mind. His human imagination takes him to Jerusalem, to the temple he knows well.

The heart of the Jewish religion and faith.

Here would be the place to make his presence known.

What was that in the psalm? God promises to protect the righteous; surely He would demonstrate that promise and protect His own Son and proclaim him Messiah.

Jesus imagines himself on the highest point of the temple where all the priests and people would see him.

If he threw himself down and the crowd saw God save his life, such drama would surely convince everyone that he was the Messiah; this would give him all the power and authority he needed to bring them into the new kingdom that his Father was offering.

But no! He knew that sensationalism had no depth whatsoever; people, no doubt, would be in awe of him and totally subjective. But fear and not love would make them conform to his message.

No, this was not the way forward.

He was fully a human being, though divine. His Father loved humanity. He must stay close to the people, share their lives, and this meant sharing their physical, spiritual and mental suffering.

He could see the way now. He was to be as vulnerable as any man or woman. He was to be their servant, show God's love and compassion and speak the truth about the new kingdom God was offering.

The devil, and his tempting thoughts, had left him but would return at a later date.

But now he could leave the desert, his mind at peace; he was resolved to show his Father's generosity and love no matter what the cost.

He was not going to use force, superhuman power or sensationalism. He would be humanity's servant. If God alone is to be worshipped and loved and all humanity made to feel at home in God's house then this was the way God's Son must choose.

12

The Wedding at Cana - John 2: 1-12

Three days later there was a wedding at Cana in Galilee. The mother of Jesus was there, and Jesus and his disciples had also been invited. When they ran out of wine, since the wine provided for the wedding was all finished, the mother of Jesus said to him, 'They have no wine.' Jesus said, 'Woman, why turn to me? My hour has not come yet.' His mother said to the servants, *'Do whatever he tells you.'* There were six stone water jars standing there, meant for the ablutions that are customary among the Jews: each could hold twenty or thirty gallons. Jesus said to the servants, 'Fill the jars with water,' and they filled them to the brim. 'Draw some out now,' he told them, 'and take it to the steward.' They did this; the steward tasted the water, and it had turned into wine. Having no idea where it came from – only the servants who had drawn the water knew – the steward called the bridegroom and said, 'People generally serve the best wine first, and keep the cheaper sort till the guests have had plenty to drink; but you have kept the best wine till now.'

This was the first of the signs given by Jesus: it was given at Cana in Galilee. He let his glory be seen, and his disciples believed in him. After this he went down to Capernaum with his mother and the brothers, but they stayed there only a few days.

❖ ❖ ❖

There is a wedding at Cana in Galilee, you have been asked to help.

The marriage ceremony is over and now everyone is outside in the sunshine.

You are standing on the edge of the large swept yard that belongs to the bride's parents.

There is music and dancing, hear the rattle of the tambourines as they bounce off the girls' hands.

You watch with pleasure as the happy couple dance together. The fringe of gold coins across the bride's brow flashes in the sun.

Their dancing comes to a happy but breathless end and they mingle with their relatives and friends.

You watch as they go to speak to a man who is standing with his mother.

You know this man; he is Jesus from Nazareth who is becoming known for his teaching.

He has influenced many people and gathered a number of men as his disciples. They are also at the wedding and are enjoying the celebrations.

Your task is to see that everyone has enough to drink. You have many wine-skins nearby which you frequently take among the people to fill their cups. Many are eager to drink; dancing in the hot sun has made them thirsty; the wine flows.

The steward, not knowing how many disciples were coming, underestimated the amount of wine needed.

You are becoming concerned because the wine-skins that lie empty far outnumber those that are full.

You begin to reduce the amount of wine and only half fill the cups.

Soon you are offering the last of the wine, and Mary the mother of Jesus is watching as you place the last empty wine-skin on the table with all the others.

Mary can see that there are no more full skins, she looks at you and your eyes meet.

You shake your head and indicate to her the empty skins lying on the table. See the limp black leather bags which still resemble the goats to which they once belonged.

You feel that she understands your concern. You feel responsible; perhaps you should not have been so generous; now you could cause embarrassment for the groom and his family through this discourtesy to their guests.

What can you do? You become alarmed when you hear Mary tell her son Jesus, 'They have no wine,' your secret is out, soon everyone will know that you have failed in your responsibilities.

Her son doesn't seem concerned, 'Woman why turn to me? My hour has not come yet.'

You are intrigued by his remark. What can he mean by 'His hour'? Does he refer to some event, which today in the middle of a wedding feast would be inappropriate?

His words sound ominous; the mystery that surrounds this man deepens.

You watch as Jesus finishes the wine in his cup and moves away.

His mother is looking at you and with a strange knowing look she says, 'Do what ever he tells you.'

Jesus is somewhere in the crowd and you are too worried to go looking for him so you return to your empty wine-skins, hoping no one will notice that the wine has stopped flowing.

The guests are still dancing, lines of men stamp the ground to the warbling pipes, and tambourines crash and beat the rhythm of the dance.

Everyone is enjoying themselves except you. They don't know that because of you the party is over.

Suddenly Jesus is standing next to you. You didn't hear his approach with all the music and singing. He puts his hand on your shoulder and you can see in his eyes that he knows how worried you are.

What he tells you to do doesn't immediately help your anxiety. Pointing to some large stone jars he tells you to fill them with water. Does he expect you to pour water instead of wine into their cups?

You remember what Mary had told you to do.

Has her son now decided that his hour has indeed come? Perhaps not where he had expected.

You do as he says and fill the jars to the brim with water drawn from the well in the corner of the yard.

You now wait for Jesus' next instruction. 'Draw some out now' he tells you.

You take a cup and dip it into the jar. 'Now take it to the steward.'

You feel very uncertain with this direction and begin to doubt these orders from Jesus.

You glance cautiously at Mary who has been watching; her eyes meet yours and they are encouraging you to do as he says.

So, you find yourself walking towards the steward, the man who hired you, with a cup of water for him to drink.

The merrymaking continues and your desperation forces you into obeying these strange orders. Added strength is given you when you remember the encouragement given by his mother. You can share her faith in her son.

You are ready to accept whatever the outcome may be.

You give the cup to the steward who gratefully accepts your service; he drinks and then looks approvingly at the cup and then to you he says, 'That is very good wine'.'

You are too relieved to speak, and the steward feels the need to congratulate the groom on providing such exceptionally good wine.

You are smiling with pleasure and great relief as you hear the steward say to the groom, 'People generally serve the best wine first, and keep the cheaper sort till the guests have had plenty to drink; but you have kept the best wine till now.'

The music and laughter have never stopped; only you and the other servants know what has just happened.

Without anyone knowing, especially the Bride and Groom, what could have been a disaster has been transformed into the manifestation of unearthly power, which has saved the day.

You look at Jesus' disciples, still enjoying the merry company, and drinking the wine which you poured from a jug filled from the water jars.

They should be told, their leader has indeed performed a miracle, and you cannot contain your rejoicing and amazement. You trusted him and he has filled your heart with gladness.

Peter and John are the nearest and are the disciples you know best.

After you have told them, they look over towards Jesus. You are surprised at their reaction. They are not excited, they have become aware of Jesus' great power to win the hearts and minds of so many people; they had suspected that even greater powers had been given to him.

Talking to the disciples has given you greater knowledge of Jesus. You want to speak to him. Firstly to thank him for saving the day, but also for more personal reasons. Today he saved you from humiliation. You are touched by his kindness; perhaps he will also understand other difficulties in your life and help you resolve them.

This day Jesus has shown that he is more than a Rabbi or Prophet; his divine power which will change the world is seen for the first time in a familiar human event and could have gone unnoticed.

13

Jesus at Nazareth – Luke 4: 16-30

He came to Nazareth, where he had been brought up, and went into the synagogue on the Sabbath day as he usually did. He stood up to read, and they handed him the scroll of the prophet Isaiah. Unrolling the scroll he found the place where it is written:

> *The spirit of the Lord has been given to me,*
> *for he has anointed me.*
> *He has sent me to bring the good news to the poor,*
> *to proclaim liberty to captives*
> *and to the blind new sight,*
> *to set the downtrodden free,*
> *to proclaim the Lord's year of favour.*

He then rolled up the scroll, gave it back to the assistant and sat down. And all eyes in the synagogue were fixed on him. Then he began to speak to them, 'This text is being fulfilled today even as you listen.' And he won the approval of all, and they were astonished by the gracious words that came from his lips.

They said, 'This is Joseph's son, surely?' But he replied, 'No doubt you will quote me the saying, "Physician, heal yourself" and tell me, "We have heard all that happened in Capernaum, do the same here in your own countryside."' And he went on, 'I tell you solemnly, no prophet is ever accepted in his own country.

'There were many widows in Israel, I can assure you, in Elijah's day, when heaven remained shut for three years and six months and a great famine raged throughout the land, but Elijah was not sent to any one of these: he was sent *to a widow at Zarephath, a Sidonian town.* And in the prophet Elisha's time there were many lepers in Israel, but none of these was cured, except the Syrian, Naaman.'

When they heard this everyone in the synagogue was enraged. They sprang to their feet and hustled him out of the town; and they took him up to the brow of the hill their town was built on, intending to throw him down the cliff, but he slipped through the crowd and walked away.

❖ ❖ ❖

Imagine that you are a resident of Nazareth, about the same age as Jesus.

You have known Jesus all your life, he was your childhood friend; you played together in the street and you were with him in Jerusalem when you were both twelve years old.

You can remember the panic he had created when his parents realized that they had left him in Jerusalem.

When you learned that they had found him in the Temple you were not surprised. He had always taken his study of scripture more seriously than the rest of his friends and was always totally absorbed in the Rabbi's words.

You know him as a young workman like yourself and have followed his progress.

He has become well-known for his teaching across the country.

Jesus at Nazareth – Luke 4: 16–30

Now you have heard that he is coming home and will be in the Synagogue on the Sabbath.

You are seated in the Synagogue, lucky to find a seat; it is full of people who like yourself have known Jesus since he was a child.

The babble of voices has stopped, the assistant has stood up, a sign for the service to begin.

He picks up the scroll which contains the Scriptures and moves towards a man sitting with the Elders.

The man stands to accept the scroll and it is now that you recognise Jesus.

He has changed, no longer the young man you know, the humble carpenter who worked with his father.

Now his presence fills the Synagogue as he confidently approaches the huge lectern in the centre of the crowded building.

There is complete silence; the people want to hear the reading but their interest in Jesus is intense, they have heard so many reports of his teaching and his healing powers.

Will their pride in him be justified?

He opens the scroll and seems to be scanning the words until he finds the place he has chosen to read.

Then he announces in a surprisingly loud clear voice that reaches every ear in the building that his reading is from the Prophet Isaiah.

He begins to read and when he looks up his face is radiant as his voice proclaims a gladness that he wants to share with his listeners.

'The spirit of the Lord has been given to me, for he has anointed me.'

He continues to read, pausing occasionally to look at the people, those listening on the floor and in the crowded gallery.

His voice rings out with a joy that you have never heard before in a man's voice.

He makes his familiar passage of Scripture come alive and penetrate your mind with new meaning.

You listen to him as you would listen to fine music, every word is pleasing in sound and meaning.

'He has sent me to bring the good news to the poor, to proclaim liberty to captives and to the blind man new sight, to set the downtrodden free, to proclaim the Lord's year of favour.'

When he has finished reading, in the complete silence all you hear is the crackle of parchment as he rolls up his scroll.

All eyes are on Jesus, in complete silence filled with expectation.

Jesus responds and standing up he begins to address the assembly.

'The promises you have just heard me read in Isaiah are today being fulfilled, and they are fulfilled in me.

'I have been given the Spirit of the Lord, at my baptism in the Jordan and while alone in the desert.

'God has anointed me to bring good news to the poor, those who cannot meet the demands of the law, those who think of themselves as inferior or unworthy.

'He gives me the power to release the prisoners of sin or ignorance.

'I can give understanding and the true meaning of the scriptures.

'The downtrodden, the marginalized will be given value they deserve as children of God.

'Yes,' he said, 'this is the year for you to receive the favour of God. I am offering you an invitation to enter the new kingdom, a kingdom of love and forgiveness.'

These are astounding words; you feel excited and the people break their attentive silence to express in hushed tones their amazement.

They are astounded; can this really be Joseph's son who they watched grow from boy to man?

Their feelings of gladness begin to fade as questions and doubts awaken as to the basis of these claims.

Jesus hears the comments, he knows these people well, he faces a crowd who will find it difficult to accept without question his prophetic claims. In their eyes he is still the town carpenter and Joseph's son.

You are ready to accept that Jesus has more to him than carpentry; you had attended seminars with him and he was always quick to grasp the deeper meaning and would surprise the Rabbi with his penetrating questions.

Jesus is aware of the change in mood and pre-empts their demand for proof.

'You will want some sign that I can put my own house in order and also that I can perform the healings I did abroad, now here in Nazareth.'

There is frozen silence when he says, 'I tell you solemnly, no prophet is ever accepted in his own country.'

They are familiar with this saying but they don't like to hear it applied to them.

The pride that had grown in their minds as a result of Jesus' reputation has changed to indignation.

Further humiliation is conferred when Jesus illustrates his point by reminding them of other prophets who were sent by God, not to Israelites like themselves but to neighbouring countries.

The mood has certainly changed, there is growing resentment. Is this man whom they watched grow up in their midst now saying that they are not capable of receiving the good news he had spoken of earlier.

They are going to teach him a lesson.

The outbreak of indignation turns to anger and produces scenes never seen in the Synagogue before.

The men push forward and roughly drag Jesus from his seat.

What they are about to do is not yet evident, but you hear the cliff mentioned. The cliff has been used before to punish people who had offended the community.

They are taking him out of the building and you follow them along the street.

You are unable to stop the angry offended men but stay close until you arrive at the cliff's edge.

You find your voice; Jesus has been your good friend from childhood, and you shout compulsively, 'He is Joseph's son, you cannot harm him, he is a Nazarene like us.'

There are angry words but the men become calmer; they release their hold and huddle into groups to vent their anger.

You catch Jesus' eye; he recognizes you and you beckon him to come while the men debate on what to do.

Quietly you both take a familiar but little used path you knew as boys, and leave unseen.

You are pleased to be close to your old friend. He seems surprisingly calm.

Now you are out of sight and safe. How good it is to be in Jesus' company. He has grown in stature but he still talks to you as a friend.

He shows great interest in you. You are glad to share with him your thoughts and feelings.

When the time comes for you to part you are glad to have deepened your friendship. You embrace each other and wish each other well.

You know that from today he will always be a big influence in your life.

14:1

The First Four Disciples are Called

– Mark 1: 16–20

As he was walking along by the Lake of Galilee, he saw Simon and Simon's brother Andrew casting a net in the lake – for they were fishermen. And Jesus said to them, 'Follow me and I will make you into fishers of men.' And at once they left their nets and followed him.

Going on a little further, he saw James, son of Zebedee, and his brother John; they too were in their boat, mending their nets. At once he called them and, leaving their father, Zebedee, in the boat with the men he employed, they went after him.

❖❖❖

Imagine Jesus walking along the banks of the beautiful Sea of Galilee: the only freshwater lake in Israel, a precious gift in a hot, dry country. It is fed by the River Jordan and lies between the hills now called the Golan Heights.

Jesus was recently baptised by John in these same waters where the Jordan leaves the lake. He then spent forty days in the

The First Four Disciples are Called - Mark 1: 16–20 & Luke 5: 1–11

hills where, overcoming temptation, he found the way forward to fulfil his life's work.

Now the time has come for action.

It is another of those warm summer days so common to this area. The water is calm; see the sun flashing on the blue surface of the water; feel the warm sun on your face.

Jesus sits down on the grassy slope to watch the fishermen working not far from the shore.

His Father has commissioned him to tell His beloved children that they are all invited into His kingdom and at last become reconciled to Him, their true Father.

Jesus is looking at one boat in particular. Two men are hauling into their boat a net full of fish. See as Jesus sees, a net full of silver, struggling fish, their flashing silver skin and flapping tails. The men cast their nets again.

Jesus is pleased to see their success; if only he could be as effective in catching the hearts and minds of his Father's children.

He continues to share their joy, and almost without thinking he shouts to the men, 'You have a good catch, you happy men, good fishing, well done. Would you be willing to fish with me, not for fish but for people?'

There was something in his voice, his demeanour, that lifted their thoughts from the fish in the boat, and sudden visions of something beyond their normal daily routine entered their minds.

The day's fishing was over. Simon, always ready to venture into a new challenge, asks the other men to secure the boat and encourages his brother Andrew to go ashore with him to find out more about this stranger and the work he has to offer.

Watch the two men as they get out of the boat and wade through the water to the lake shore, where Jesus greets them and shakes their hand.

The three men are now walking along the shore of the lake in the evening sunlight. Other boats are bringing in their catch, but some have sent their catch to market and now sit in their boats, mending nets.

Jesus sees two young men sitting in their father's boat, mending nets as usual after a day's fishing. Impulsively, Jesus feels it would be right to invite these men to be his helpers in the task ahead. He cannot do it alone.

The brothers see Jesus, and Simon and Andrew standing on the shore, and James and John stop their mending.

'If you follow me,' Jesus says, 'I will make you into fishers of men.'

The two brothers have known Simon and Andrew since childhood and have grown up together in the fishing village. Simon has always been the leader and they have shared many an adventure in the past; this could turn out to be another.

Their father, Zebedee, hears what Jesus is saying but is more concerned with repairing his nets and lets his sons go off. They will be safe with Simon, whoever the stranger might be.

So the five of them move off together, a good day's work behind all of them.

As they walk they discover that this stranger has some interesting ideas and they soon take a liking to him.

They continue to walk together, and as they listen to Jesus talking about the prophets and the scriptures they are beginning to leave their old lives behind and are now willing to enter the biggest adventure of their lives. Where will this man lead them?

14:2

The First Four Disciples are Called – Luke 5: 1–11

Now he was standing one day by the lake of Gennesaret, with the crowd pressing round him listening to the word of God, when he caught sight of two boats close to the bank. The fishermen had gone out of them and were washing their nets. He got into one of the boats – it was Simon's – and asked him to put out a little from the shore. Then he sat down and taught the crowds from the boat.

When he had finished speaking he said to Simon, 'Put out into deep water and pay out your nets for a catch.' 'Master,' Simon replied, 'we worked hard all night long and caught nothing, but if you say so, I will pay out the nets.' And when they had done this they netted such a huge number of fish that their nets began to tear, so they signalled to their companions in the other boat to come and help them; when these came, they filled the two boats to sinking point.

When Simon Peter saw this, he fell at the knees of Jesus saying, 'Leave me, Lord; I am a sinful man.' For he and all his companions were completely overcome by the catch they had made; so also were James and John, sons of Zebedee, who were Simon's partners. But Jesus said to Simon, 'Do not be afraid; from now on it is men you will catch.' Then bringing their boats back to land, they left everything and followed him.

❖❖❖

The sun beats down from a clear blue sky, the lake is calm and reflects the sky like blue satin.

A large crowd is gathered on its grassy banks, and Jesus can hardly be seen in their midst.

He is trying to make his voice heard over the people's heads.

The longer he speaks the closer the crowd gets, hungry to hear more, not wanting to miss a single word.

They cannot be held back and a wall of people now surrounds him, a barrier to his words.

Over their shoulders he can see below the peaceful lake so different from the stifling crowd that surrounds him.

He catches sight of two fishing boats half beached on the narrow shore.

How good it would be to leave the crowd and the shore in one of these boats; he could still talk to them, the water would carry his voice.

He continues to talk to the eager listeners but his eyes search for the men who might own the boats.

He sees them near the boats washing their nets and he recognises Simon.

This encourages him because Simon has become a friend.

Jesus stops talking and the crowd look in the direction of his gaze.

The First Four Disciples are Called - Mark 1: 16–20 & Luke 5: 1–11

He moves forward and the crowd part to let him pass.

Such is the respect the crowd have for him, no one tries to stop his progress to the lakeside.

When he gets there he stands to watch Simon washing his nets, an honest workman in his eyes.

Simon looks up and now follows Jesus' gaze towards his boats and stops his work.

Jesus has climbed into one of them and looks towards Simon.

'Simon will you take me into the lake a little distance from the shore?'

Simon jumps to his feet, collects his nets and places them in the boat.

He gladly responds to his request and takes Jesus a little way from the shore.

Jesus now sits down and again addresses the crowd who now fill the shoreline and the hillside.

Simon has anchored the boat and sits listening to Jesus' words.

Jesus brings his talk to an end; the people softly call down blessings upon him.

He looks into the boat and sees Simon's empty nets, no sign of fish in the boat or on shore.

'Put out into deep water and pay out your nets for a catch,' says Jesus.

Simon doesn't respond in his usual manner; this is unexpected.

'Master we worked hard all night long and caught nothing, but if you say so, I will pay out the nets.'

He has seen the power of Jesus when he cured a member of his family.

He complains no more and rows out into deeper water.

He stops rowing and carries out Jesus' orders, not without some doubt still remaining.

He hurls the nets into the water which hisses and foams as they sink.

Time to haul them in, they are heavy, very heavy. His eyes are wide open in disbelief; the nets are full to bursting.

His excitement nearly makes him lose his grip but he recovers enough to bring the precious catch into the boat.

He casts again, even more fish than before and the nets begin to tear.

He must call for help; James and John hear his calls and bring their boat.

Net after net fill their boats with fish until the boats are in danger of sinking.

In all the activity Simon has forgotten Jesus, but now as he rests from his labours he sees Jesus smiling at him from the stern.

The mystery is compounded that surrounds this man. Simon begins to feel fear.

Should he, a simple fisherman, be associated with such a powerful man?

He falls to his knees among the fish and with fear in his voice he begs Jesus to leave him; he feels so unworthy of his friendship and out of his depth.

James and John have become still, sharing the moment.

The First Four Disciples are Called - Mark 1: 16–20 & Luke 5: 1-11

There is silence now, only the gentle rocking of the boats and soft waves lap the wooden sides.

They wait, and the peace is filled when Jesus calms their fears. 'Do not be afraid; from now on it is men you will catch'.

They all look at the people still waiting on the shore. They now feel a different excitement, not from personal gain but a new gladness which comes from serving a great man.

15

Jesus and the Pharisees – Luke 5: 27–39 and 6: 1–5

When he went out after this, he noticed a tax collector, Levi by name, sitting by the customs house, and said to him, 'Follow me.' And leaving everything he got up and followed him.

In his honour Levi held a great reception in his house, and with them at table was a large gathering of tax collectors and others. The Pharisees and their scribes complained to his disciples and said, 'Why do you eat and drink with tax collectors and sinners?' Jesus said to them in reply, 'It is not those who are well who need the doctor, but the sick. I have not come to call the virtuous, but sinners to repentance.'

They then said to him, 'John's disciples are always fasting and saying prayers, and the disciples of the Pharisees too, but yours go on eating and drinking.' Jesus replied, 'Surely you cannot make the bridegroom's attendants fast while the bridegroom is still with them? But the time will come, the time for the bridegroom to be taken away from them; that will be the time when they will fast.'

He also told them this parable, 'No one tears a piece from a new cloak to put it on an old cloak; if he does, not only will he have torn the new one, but the piece taken from the new will not match the old.

'And nobody puts new wine into old skins; if he does, the new wine will burst the skins and then run out, and the skins will be lost. No; new wine must be put into fresh skins. And nobody who has been drinking old wine wants new. "The old is good" he says.'

Now one sabbath he happened to be taking a walk through the cornfields, and his disciples were picking ears of corn, rubbing them in their hands and eating them. Some of the Pharisees said, 'Why are you doing something that is forbidden on the sabbath day?' Jesus answered them, 'So you have not read what David did when he and his followers were hungry – how he went into the house of God, took the loaves of offering and ate them and gave them to his followers, loaves which only the priests are allowed to eat?' And he said to them, 'The Son of Man is master of the sabbath.'

❖❖❖

Imagine that you are a tax collector in Israel at the time of Jesus.

You are employed by the Romans to collect money from your own people to support the occupying army and the general maintenance of the country.

Jesus has invited you to be one of his close followers; you are surprised and delighted. The burden of a rather ignoble occupation has been lifted and the door has been opened for you to enter what Jesus calls a New Kingdom.

You have a reputation for exactitude and cold efficiency but now you generously want to share the great gift Jesus is offering.

You have decided to create a gathering where all your colleagues and others who might feel outcasts from society can share the joy that has been given to you.

A meal has been prepared; you want it to be a feast to celebrate the dawn of what promises to be a new life for everyone.

The meal is a success, the food and wine excellent. You are not disappointed in any way. All the invited guests feel the beneficence of Jesus' words and actions and like yourself they can now see themselves in a different light.

They feel accepted and loved by God no matter what others might think.

The evening is over, the guests feel satisfied not only with good food but an inner contentment floods them with a reassurance and a peace never felt before.

Jesus' words were rich nourishment that satisfied deep longings.

You are now standing at the door with Jesus by your side saying goodbye to your guests. Many shake hands with Jesus and also thank you for your hospitality.

There are some onlookers and among them you see some Pharisees and their scribes who seem to be taking notes of their observations.

The Pharisees come up to you, and while Jesus is involved with the parting guests, they ask him with a note of reproach more than enquiry, 'Why do you eat and drink with tax collectors and sinners?'

The convivial atmosphere of the occasion is chilled by their veiled condemnation and air of disapproval.

Jesus answers them, 'It is not those who are well who need the doctor, but the sick, I have not come to call the virtuous, but sinners to repentance.'

His words opened your eyes to the difference between the attitude of the Pharisees and the attitude of you and your colleagues.

Jesus and the Pharisees - Luke 5: 27-39 and 6: 1-5

Your feelings of guilt and rejection had been lifted, but the Pharisees had never felt guilty because they kept the law and through their good behaviour they considered themselves pleasing to God. Their own actions achieved salvation.

The Pharisees are silenced but follow you and Jesus as you leave the house.

A voice comes from behind, 'Why don't you and your disciples fast and pray as John's disciples do and as we do? John's disciples fast and pray, we only see yours eating and drinking.'

The hairs stand up on the back of your neck; you resent this insolent challenge.

Jesus has stopped and he turns to face the Pharisees who wait with a sly amused expression in their faces.

There is no anger in Jesus' voice as he explains to them that people can be relaxed and happy at gatherings such as a wedding because the bridegroom is still with them; when he is gone is the time to fast and pray. His own presence in the world is a cause for celebration.

Jesus opens again the door into his new kingdom which is quite different from the world of the Pharisees. His new world cannot be grafted onto the old one, being totally different.

They stop following you, still not understanding the depth of the words they are hearing.

It is now the Sabbath day and you are walking with Jesus and the other disciples outside the town among the corn fields.

The sun shines out of a serenely blue sky. Feel the sun's warmth on your face as you enjoy this day in the company of Jesus.

Blood red poppies playfully decorate the straight uniform stalks of corn. Their heavy ears of swollen grain sway in graceful waves across the golden field. The corn's sun-warmed breath fills the air and the heat haze blurs the distant view.

Black swallows glide and swoop in reckless flight over the golden crop.

You have never walked in these fields before and Jesus' love of the world has opened your eyes to its beauty.

You have never felt so content; Jesus has invited you all into a family; you all come from various backgrounds but all differences are forgotten and your devotion to Jesus unites everyone.

Being with Jesus makes your life a continual celebration. This feeling of contentment and peace is sublime and will remain with you forever.

All your senses are replete as you stroke the rough ears of corn along the edge of the field bordered by a low stone wall.

You break off an ear of corn and rub it between your hands.

Feel the coarse husks on your palms as they release the grain. When you blow on your hands the husks fly away and you eat the corn seeds.

Into your newly found world others with different values have strayed. The Pharisees have found you and want to pursue their questioning.

They remind you that it is the Sabbath Day and you are picking and eating corn which is against the law.

You have no answer nor do you feel like justifying your behaviour; you no longer care what they think; the Bridegroom is surely with you, nothing else matters.

But Jesus, who enjoys debates, responds by reminding them that David with his followers ate the sacred bread in the Temple and broke the law.

They have no reply to give and in the silence, there amid the corn fields Jesus makes an earth moving claim, 'The Son of Man is master of the Sabbath,' and you know that he is declaring himself to be greater than any law.

The Pharisees retreat once more and you, Jesus and the disciples continue your walk among the corn fields rejoicing in your new freedom.

16

Cure of the Man with a Withered Hand
~ Luke 6: 6-11

Now on another Sabbath he went into the synagogue and began to teach, and a man was there whose right hand was withered. The scribes and the Pharisees were watching him to see if he would cure a man on the Sabbath, hoping to find something to use against him. But he knew their thoughts; and he said to the man with the withered hand, 'Stand up! Come out into the middle.' And he came out and stood there. Then Jesus said to them, 'I put it to you: is it against the law on the Sabbath to do good, or to do evil; to save life, or to destroy it?' Then he looked round at them all and said to the man, 'Stretch out your hand.' He did so, and his hand was better. But they were furious, and began to discuss the best way of dealing with Jesus.

❖❖❖

And now I ask you dear reader to take the part of the man who sits in the Synagogue this Sabbath morning.

Your right hand has been useless since birth, the muscles are wasted and weak and you always carry it inside your tunic where its deformity cannot be seen.

Cure of the Man with a Withered Hand – Luke 6: 6–11

The Pharisees who belong to your Synagogue have suggested that you should sit where Jesus will notice you when he is teaching this Sabbath.

You are not comfortable with their suggestion and rather suspect their motives.

Having heard of Jesus curing people it has only been a vague hope that one day he might heal you.

You agree to do what they suggest, but the Synagogue is not the place you would have chosen to ask for Jesus' healing powers, being far too public.

So now you are sitting in the Synagogue which is full of people. You have only half complied with the Pharisees' wishes and you sit at the back where you may not be noticed so easily.

You now look at Jesus sitting with the Pharisees and Elders; his teaching is new and has stirred thoughts that are leading you into a different relationship with God. The old relationship where God demanded perfection and strict adherence to the law has changed. Now Jesus wants you to think of God as a Father who loves and accepts you unconditionally.

Your heart warms towards this man and when you look at the Pharisees their cold watchful eyes show no love or respect; you are disturbed and don't want to be a pawn in their underhand schemes.

Now you are glad not to have fully co-operated with them.

But you stop breathing when you see that Jesus notices that the Pharisees are looking in your direction.

He follows their gaze and he has stopped talking at the great lectern.

There is complete silence and all wait. He is now looking straight at you; he suspects that you have some connection with the Pharisees.

Then to your intense embarrassment you hear him call you out from the back row and into the front where everyone can see you, 'Stand up! Come out into the middle.' All eyes turn on you as you make your way through the people.

Your quick glance at the Pharisees shows you that this is what they have been waiting for.

You are now standing in the middle of the Synagogue surrounded by your amazed fellow countrymen who have all started to mutter and question each other. This has never happened during a service before.

You are standing close to Jesus and you forget your acute embarrassment because his warm compassionate nature has evoked a feeling of wellbeing and gladness; the watching eyes and muttered disapprovals all fade away.

You stand, your withered hand hidden, and Jesus places his hand on your shoulder and asks the crowd, 'Is it against the law on the Sabbath to do good, or to do evil; to save life, or to destroy it?'

The Pharisees look uncomfortable and the crowd respond timidly agreeing that life is better than death, good better than evil any day of the week.

Your embarrassment returns when Jesus asks you to take your misshapen hand from its hiding place and stretch it out for all to see.

You have always kept it out of sight even when you are with family or friends.

Cure of the Man with a Withered Hand – Luke 6: 6–11

Slowly you remove it from your tunic and extend your arm out, your hand exposed.

Nobody has seen it before and there are some gasps as the twisted knotted fingers and the withered muscles are now the attention of all eyes.

Jesus' hand still rests on your shoulder and you feel a warmth move down your arm and into your hand.

The distorted muscles relax their crippling hold, the contorted fingers become straight and your hand is filled with strength and movement.

The feeling of wellbeing you experienced earlier has turned into a joy you could never have imagined.

Your family and friends are on their feet, tears in many eyes as they come to share your happiness and also to wonder at Jesus and his astounding powers. But it is his compassion for you that impresses them greatly and their thanks are beyond words.

You look from your healed hand to Jesus and feel rather unworthy of his great kindness; you are here today in league with the Pharisees.

But as you see the Pharisees leave the building unhappy that their plans have failed, you know now where your loyalties lie.

Jesus has confounded their deviousness with his open forthright ways. From your hidden shame he has brought you into the freedom of his love.

17

The Call of Levi - Luke 6: 27-28

When Jesus went out after this, he noticed a tax collector, Levi by name, sitting by the customs house, and said to him, 'Follow me.' And leaving everything he got up and followed him.

❖❖❖

Levi the tax collector sits alone by the Customs house watching the people in the street.

Sad thoughts are invading his mind, which force him to consider his way of life.

He looks at the people in the street, sees them talking in groups, some buying food for their families.

Children playing together under the watchful gaze of their mothers, who sit in the market square.

He could be invisible, no one gives him any recognition, and he knows if he offered a greeting it would not be returned.

He has reached maturity, but what does he have to call his own? Money has been his only reason for living. He has it locked away in the Customs house and counts it often.

The Call of Levi - Luke 6: 27-28

But this pleasure has faded of late, which makes his life feel empty.

He has tried to overcome these unwelcome thoughts but today he feels his loneliness is increased in spite of the busy scene before him.

He reminds himself again of all his money, and how he often counts it before he returns to his large, well furnished house alone.

He has no family, what Jewish woman would marry him?

His emptiness is increased as he watches the children play; some look at him with their dark eyes as they hold tight their mother's hand.

He finds fleeting comfort in their non-judgemental gaze, but mothers will pull them away.

He will never have children, and his hoard of gold is cold comfort when deep human longings fill his heart.

His youth is long gone, is money to be his only companion? His life is dedicated in service to wealth, has he become a slave?

He remembers the friends he had when young; where are they all? The childhood sweetheart he has never forgotten. He sees her often but she keeps her children away from him.

He may have nephews and nieces but the family disown him and the next generation will not know him.

Why these thoughts? Where are they coming from? Gold is what he wanted so why this sadness? He feels the poorest man on earth.

He feels unloved and even worse, he has no one to love.

An overwhelming feeling of guilt also compounds his darkness; he has been a traitor to his own people and served their enemy.

No one will care for him when he is old. He has never felt so vulnerable.

His mind searches desperately for an answer, or someone who can help him. There is no one at the Customs house, his family are strangers to him, fellow tax collectors would despise his weakness.

His anguish overwhelms him, there is nowhere to turn for help.

A gentle voice speaks his name, 'Levi.' He doesn't lift his head, no one ever speaks to him, but again he hears, 'Levi,' and he looks up into the face of Jesus and time stands still. All the demons that once threatened his sanity are now dispelled.

He looks into Jesus' eyes and they remind him of a child, free from judgement, but most wonderful is his look of concern, and concern for him and him alone as he says, 'I will be your rock, a sure foundation; come follow me.'

Jesus helps him to his feet, and Levi takes hold of his arms for support and to confirm that Jesus is flesh and blood.

A wonderful peace now fills his whole being; the abyss has been taken away, he is safe.

His head rests now on Jesus' breast and his hidden tears fall.

Levi's heart is broken, but the peace he now has is worth all the gold he could ever possess.

He accepts with gladness Jesus' offer and leaves the Customs house forever.

18

Cure of the Centurion's Servant - Luke 7: 1-10

When he had come to the end of all he wanted the people to hear, he went into Capernaum. A centurion there had a servant, a favourite of his, who was sick and near death. Having heard about Jesus he sent some Jewish Elders to him to ask him to come and heal his servant. When they came to Jesus they pleaded earnestly with him, 'He deserves this of you,' they said, 'because he is friendly towards our people, in fact, he is the one who built the synagogue.' So Jesus went with them, and was not very far from the house when the centurion sent word to him by some friends. 'Sir,' he said, 'do not put yourself to trouble; because I am not worthy to have you under my roof; and for this same reason I did not presume to come to you myself; but give the word and let my servant be cured. For I am under authority myself, and have soldiers under me; and I say to one man. Go, and he goes, to another, Come here, and he comes; to my servant; Do this, and he does it.' When Jesus heard these words he was astonished at him and, turning round, said to the crowd following him, 'I tell you, not even in Israel have I found faith like this.' And when the messengers got back to the house they found the servant in perfect health.

❖❖❖

Can you see this Centurion who is living in Capernaum, a strong competent leader of men? He commands a well disciplined regiment who respect and obey him. His men are loyal because his judgement is sound and his orders are clear.

But what has sealed their respect is his humanity and his concern for his men, not only in battle but also in their private lives.

His concern is not confined to his regiment but also to the people who live in Capernaum whose religion he has come to respect.

Some of his fellow officers criticise him for "going native". But when he instigates the building of a Synagogue and funds its construction the compatibility between the army and the Jewish people is unique in Israel.

He was a man who possessed authority and compassion.

A man who has served him loyally for many years has become seriously ill, all treatment has failed and he is dying.

The Centurion has heard many people talk about the man from Nazareth and has liked what he heard. He sounds different from the other religious leaders; this man lives for others and not for self aggrandizement. He can also identify with someone who acknowledges that they receive their authority from a greater power than themselves.

The Centurion is also a good judge of men and he has great respect for Jesus; and like the bright sun suddenly appearing from behind a black cloud he feels certain that this man can cure his servant.

But he is not a Jew, and there is a risk that Jesus will not be concerned with someone outside Judaism.

Cure of the Centurion's Servant - Luke 7: 1-10

Perhaps there will be a greater possibility of him helping his servant if Jesus is asked by Jewish Elders.

The Centurion has no difficulty in getting the Elders of the Synagogue to go on his behalf and out of gratitude and respect they take his request for help to Jesus.

When they find Jesus they surprise him by their earnest pleading for him to answer the request from a Roman soldier.

Jesus has never seen such generous compatibility between his fellow countrymen and their pagan rulers.

They tell Jesus, 'He deserves this of you because he is friendly towards our people, in fact, he is the one who built the Synagogue.'

Jesus senses that this Centurion is not merely occupied with law and order and suppression, but through his humanity he has brought a rare peace to Capernaum.

His heart warms towards this Roman and he agrees to accompany the Elders who lead him to the dying servant.

As the Centurion waits, he has some misgivings and regrets asking Jesus to come to his home; he is aware of a greater authority than his own, and a power unrestricted by human conditions. There is no need for Jesus to come to his servant because he serves an omnipotent God.

He hastily asks a friend of the family to go and meet Jesus on the way and say to him, 'Sir do not put yourself to trouble; because I am not worthy to have you under my roof; and for this same reason I did not presume to come to you myself; but give the word and let my servant be cured. For I am under authority myself, and have soldiers under me; and I say to one man; Go, and he goes; to another, Come here and he comes; to my servant do this and he does it.'

Jesus is astonished when he hears such respect especially from a Roman soldier.

He instantly feels a strong bond with this man even though they come from very different backgrounds.

Jesus' heart rejoices and he turns to share his happiness with the following crowd and says, 'I tell you, not even in Israel have I found faith like this.'

The two men never meet, but as the Centurion sits beside his loyal servant he can see a remarkable change come over him. The servant sits up and drinks some water and even asks for food.

Jesus has answered his request and as he gazes out of the window over the town of Capernaum, he knows that out there is a truly remarkable man who has power, authority and great compassion. Dare he think that his own benign authority could possibly stem from the same compassionate God whom Jesus serves?

Even though they may never meet there will always be a bond between them which fills his heart with gladness and unbounded gratitude.

19

The Woman who was a Sinner - Luke 7: 36-50

One of the Pharisees invited him to a meal. When he arrived at the Pharisee's house and took his place at the table, a woman came in, who had a bad name in the town. She had heard he was dining with the Pharisee and had brought with her an alabaster jar of ointment. She waited behind him at his feet, weeping, and her tears fell on his feet, and she wiped them away with her hair; then she covered his feet with her kisses and anointed them with the ointment.

When the Pharisee who had invited him saw this, he said to himself, 'If this man were a prophet, he would know who this woman is that is touching him and what a bad name she has.' Then Jesus took him up and said, 'Simon I have something to say to you.' 'Speak Master,' was the reply. 'There once was a creditor who had two men in his debt, one owed him five hundred denarii, the other fifty. They were unable to pay, so he pardoned them both. Which of them will love him more?' 'The one who was pardoned more, I suppose,' answered Simon. Jesus said, 'You are right.' Then he turned to the woman, 'Simon,' he said, 'you see this woman? I came into your house, and you poured no water over my feet, but she has poured out her tears over my feet and wiped them away with her hair. You gave me no kiss, but she has been covering my feet with kisses ever since I came in. You did not anoint my head with oil, but she has anointed my feet with ointment. For this reason I tell you that her sins, her many sins, must have been forgiven her, or she would not have shown such great love. It is the man who is forgiven little who shows little love.' Then he said to her, 'Your sins are forgiven.' Those who were with him at the table began to say to themselves, 'Who is this man, that he even forgives sins?' But he said to the woman, 'Your faith has saved you; go in peace.'

❖❖❖

Can you see a woman sitting alone in a room which she rents in the poorer district of the town?

Her room is simple, the emphasis is on comfort, and attempts at luxury, with large colourful cushions and curtains that hide the crumbling walls.

She sits with her hands clasped on her knees, her face is composed, a stillness is upon her.

She feels a great change has come upon her since she heard the man from Nazareth speak in the market place.

He had spoken of a jealous God who loved her in a way no man had ever loved her.

When Jesus had looked at her, in his eyes there was neither contempt nor the desire which she usually received from men. This man's love is different and it has changed her.

She now feels valued and worthy of a better life. She wants to be worthy of a place in the new kingdom which Jesus offers her.

She must put her life in order and be free of her sinful ways. His love has opened her eyes and enables her to make a new life for herself.

The Woman who was a Sinner - Luke 7: 36–50

Before he leaves this town there is something she must do, her heart being as it is so full of love, a love that fills her with joy and not shame.

She must see him and in some way show her love and gratitude.

She sees an unopened alabaster box of ointment ready for use on her clients; it will now be used in an act which will transform her life forever.

She removes her bracelets and bangles, her ornate earrings and the heavy seductive make-up.

With her head covered she leaves her house carrying the precious jar hidden in her clothing. She knows where she will find the source of her newly found gladness and she must thank him.

Picture now the room in Simon the Pharisee's house; a long low table is covered with plates of food, bowls of fruit and cups of wine.

Many men lie on cushions beside the table; the host is at the head and at the other end Jesus is reclining as he eats and talks to the men on either side.

Simon talks with some animation to the men, but as he speaks his eyes are upon Jesus at the other end of the table.

His interest in Jesus is growing but he is not prepared to let this be known to others and therefore keeps him at a distance where he can observe him but not become involved.

But now he has stopped listening to the men talking to him because his full attention is given to Jesus.

He notices a figure kneeling behind Jesus near to his feet.

He didn't recognise her at first; this now quiet respectful figure contrasts with the attention seeking seductive woman he knows her to be. Her downcast eyes that once flashed at men are now full of tears.

What can this mean? Normally he would have had her thrown out but tonight she seems a very different person.

This also could be a good testing ground for Jesus and Simon will be very interested to see how he handles the situation.

The woman however remains unnoticed by the other men and she is left in peace to pay homage to the only man in the world that has made her feel loved and forgiven and valued above everything else on earth.

She is surprised by the tears that fill her eyes, her heart is full of love and a strange sadness. She is forgiven and loved unconditionally, her gratitude is profound.

Jesus is still unaware of her at his feet and continues talking with the other guests while the tears roll down the woman's cheeks and drop onto his feet.

She lets her warm tears wash his feet and they express what is in her heart better than any words.

She gently removes her light shawl and uses her long hair to dry Jesus' feet.

Jesus becomes aware of her and their eyes meet; again she feels loved and accepted by him as he allows her to show her gratitude and homage in the only way she can.

Encouraged and unafraid she now bends lower and kisses Jesus' feet, a humble act of love and her childlike affection is unrestrained.

She now reveals the jar of ointment, and glad of this wonderful opportunity she removes the lid and covers Jesus' feet with the sweet smelling unction.

Her hands perform a wonderful act, one that says so much and will redeem her life.

Simon has been watching closely and is puzzled by Jesus' behaviour; he must know who this woman is even though the gaudy make-up and cheap jewellery are gone. But Simon also sees the tears and the once arrogant flamboyance replaced with quiet humility.

Even so, a true Prophet would not let himself be contaminated by such a woman.

Jesus is aware of the critical look in Simon's eyes and says, 'Simon, I have something to say to you,' and Simon now eager to hear, 'Speak master,' he replies.

'There was once a creditor,' says Jesus, 'who had two men in his debt; one owed him five hundred denarii, the other fifty. They were unable to pay, so he pardoned them both. Which of them will love him more?'

'The one who was pardoned more, I suppose,' answered Simon, trying to appear indifferent. 'You are right,' says Jesus.

He turns to look at the woman at his feet who is now sitting on the floor content to be near him.

'Simon,' he says, 'you see this woman? I came into your house, and you poured no water over my feet, but she has poured out her tears over my feet and wiped them away with her hair. You gave me no kiss, but she has been covering my feet with kisses ever since I came in. You did not anoint my head with oil, but she has anointed my feet with ointment. For this reason I tell you that her sins, her many sins, must have been forgiven her, or she would not have shown such great love. It is the man who is forgiven little who shows little love.'

Simon and the other guests are silenced by Jesus' words. How can he honour such a woman, and even elevate her in such a way? But they must admit, if only to themselves, that a great change has taken place and they can see a joy and peace in her face which they would dearly like to share. A sense of poverty fills them with a longing that reminds them of their childhood.

Jesus turns to her again and confirms her trust in him, 'Your sins are indeed forgiven.'

She has accomplished what she set out to do and now feels self-conscious for the first time since she entered the room.

All eyes are upon her but her peace remains.

As she looks into Jesus' eyes for the last time, she finds an intimacy that satisfies her deepest longing.

Guests hide their embarrassment and loudly express their indignation for anyone who professes an ability to forgive sins.

Their feeling of poverty and longing reminded them of childhood, but the cost of abandoning their own righteousness is too high, and so they remain apart.

Many would like to share the child like happiness they can see in this woman and they could be shown the way when they hear Jesus tell her, 'Your faith has saved you, go in peace.'

She has indeed found peace and a man who is safe to love; he will never let her down, she can now grow into the woman she was born to be.

20

The Cure of Simon Peter's Mother-in-law – Mark 1: 29–31

And at once on leaving the synagogue, he went with James and John straight to the house of Simon and Andrew. Now Simon's mother-in-law was in bed and feverish, and at once they told him about her. He went in to her, took her by the hand and helped her up. And the fever left her and she began to serve them.

❖❖❖

Picture Jesus as he leaves the synagogue with his disciples.

There are James and John, Peter and Andrew. You are with them as a friend.

His disciples look thoughtful, and not much is being said.

They have just seen Jesus show the power he has to heal a deranged man in the synagogue. They had never seen anyone do this before.

Even more astounding had been hearing Jesus reading from the scriptures and claiming himself to be the fulfilment of Isaiah's prophecy, and that he is the anointed one promised by God.

It's been a long day.

You hear Peter inviting him and the others to his home for something to eat.

Jesus accepts, and Peter leads everyone through the narrow streets. Hear the street noises.

Watch the people as you walk along the road. Men selling fruit. Women with children. Carpet sellers calling people to buy.

Some children playing in a doorway. A man leading a donkey carrying firewood.

You now see Peter go towards a doorway in the street and invite you all in.

The first person you see is Peter's wife. She looks pale and anxious.

As you enter the living room she tells Jesus that her mother has been ill all night and since Peter left she has become delirious.

You look around the room and notice the table is covered with dirty plates, there is no fire in the grate and the curtains are not open.

You can see that Peter is embarrassed; this is poor hospitality, and hospitality is very important in his culture.

He explains to Jesus that his wife has been nursing her mother all day, and had no time to prepare for his visit.

Peter remembers the way Jesus cured the man in the synagogue.

The Cure of Simon Peter's Mother-in-law – Mark 1: 29–31

With reverence and great respect he asks Jesus if he could help his mother-in-law.

Without any hesitation you see Jesus accompany Peter into the bedroom. You follow.

There you see the old lady, in bed, her daughter beside her.

The old lady is restless, beads of sweat on her pale forehead and on her upper lip.

She is muttering incoherently.

Her hands clutch at the bedclothes; her eyes are open and frightened.

You watch Jesus move towards the bed. He bends over the old lady, he takes her restless hand and at once a stillness comes over her.

She is restless no more. She holds onto Jesus' hand; her eyes, now calm again, look into his.

Her eyes are fixed on him until she is completely calm. Her breathing is now slower. She smiles at Jesus.

He smiles back. Colour comes back to her cheeks.

She says, 'You must be the man Peter has been talking about.'

You see the relief on her daughter's face as she embraces Peter and her mother.

Peter now turns to Jesus and with intense wonder and gratitude he kisses Jesus' hand.

Who or what is this man who has such astonishing powers? What is such a man doing in his humble home? How could he be of any use to a man such as Jesus? Why has Jesus made him a close friend? It has all happened so quickly.

While everyone is expressing wonder and thanks, you see that the old lady has got up and dressed herself.

Now she feels so well and full of life, she must do something.

She lights the fire. Hear it crackle, see the smoke.

She tells her daughter to tidy the table and chairs.

She goes and brings food and drink and puts it on the table.

Peter is now full of gladness; his home is back to normal.

But he senses his life is changing; things are not going to be the same, because of his friendship with Jesus.

His mother-in-law brings more food to the table.

You watch Jesus enjoying the hospitality. He is quite at home in the middle of the family.

There is a lot to talk about as they all sit and eat by the fire.

You look at Peter. He is looking at Jesus and seems lost in his thoughts; what could those thoughts be? What is he thinking?

21

Jesus Quietly Leaves Capernaum and Travels Through Galilee – Mark 1: 35–39

In the morning, long before dawn, he got up and left the house and went off to a lonely place and prayed there. Simon and his companions set out in search of him, and when they found him they said, 'Everybody is looking for you.' He answered, 'Let us go elsewhere, to the neighbouring country towns, so that I can proclaim the message there too, because that is why I came.' And he went all through Galilee, preaching in their synagogues and driving out devils.

❖❖❖

Imagine you are one of the disciples of Jesus, and you are with him in Capernaum on the shores of the Sea of Galilee.

Yesterday had been another busy day. Hundreds of people had been in and around the house, wanting Jesus.

Ever since you arrived in Capernaum Jesus had preached to the crowds, telling them that they were all forgiven and God, their loving Father, was inviting them into His new kingdom.

He had shown great compassion for the poor and the sick: many had been cured; even more had been heartened by his good news.

It's early morning. You have slept well, but now there is a commotion outside your window. You can hear many voices. You know they are calling for Jesus.

The sun hasn't risen yet, but you can see a soft blue mist waiting to be soon melted by the sun.

You get out of the bed and put some clothes on, and go to the door where someone is knocking.

You are feeling rather annoyed, you resent their impatience; don't they have any consideration for Jesus, coming this early in the morning?

You can see the other disciples are also up and getting dressed.

You open the door; dozens of faces confront you, all asking for Jesus. When you see their careworn faces, the sick, the cripples, your annoyance fades. You are already beginning to share in Jesus' compassion for the people; the poor and the sick were not your concern before.

You have no choice, you must find Jesus; you turn to go and look for him.

You know where he will be; he likes to sleep on the flat roof where he can see the stars.

You go through to the back of the house where the outside steps lead onto the roof. You climb each step, thinking it unusual for Jesus not to be up before everyone else. You are on the roof

Jesus Quietly Leaves Capernaum/Travels Through Galilee – Mark 1: 35–39

of the house; you can hear the crowd below. Jesus is not here; his bed is empty.

You feel stunned. Where is he? Did you miss him downstairs? You go back down into the house but others haven't seen Jesus either.

The crowd has grown even more; they are sitting down and refuse to move until Jesus comes out to speak to them.

Simon, who owns the house, says Jesus must be found. He will go to the synagogue, other disciples to friends' houses, but he tells you to go and search up the hill behind the house.

You quietly slip away from the house through the back door so that no one will see you.

The sun is just beginning to light the sky over the hills, the gold light reflected on the water below. The air is warming and the sun is melting the mist over the still blue waters of the lake.

You keep climbing the dry stony hill; you enjoy the peace of the early morning as you climb higher and higher away from the noisy crowd below.

You are at the top at last and there you see a figure sitting cross-legged on the ground. You have found him. You know from the tranquillity of the scene that he is praying.

You stop where you are and go no nearer; you know how much he values time to pray, how important it is to him. Now it is becoming an important part of your life also.

You also sit on the dry, stony ground and share this tranquil moment with Jesus.

Jesus looks up and sees you sitting there a short distance from him.

He greets you by your name. He looks pleased to have your company; you're not intruding. Your heart warms towards him as always.

'Master,' you say, 'We all need you at Peter's house. The crowds are there already and won't leave until you speak to them.'

Jesus gazes down the hillside towards the house. He can hear the people. His compassion shows on his face, but he makes no move to go down to them.

You hear footsteps behind you. At first you think it must be the people, but when you turn to look you see Peter and the rest of the disciples coming up the hill towards you.

When they get near they say, 'Master, everyone is looking for you.'

Jesus still remains seated, then he says, 'It's time to move on and go to the other towns in Galilee. I must preach there as well, for that is why I am here.'

Jesus is not going to return to the crowd outside Peter's home. Peter's wife and mother-in-law will have to deal with the people as best they can.

You must move on with Jesus, there is no going back. Even though it may not feel the right thing to do. You are letting a lot of people down.

But your devotion and faith in Jesus has grown so much you can accept these sudden, unexpected moves. You had left your fishing boat just as suddenly and had never regretted it.

Jesus gets to his feet and turns to walk down the other side of the hill. You and the rest of the disciples only have the clothes you are standing in, but you know that all your needs will be met. Jesus is often saying not to worry about food and clothing; there are more important things to think about.

Jesus Quietly Leaves Capernaum/Travels Through Galilee – Mark 1: 35–39

You enjoy the sense of freedom and you gladly follow him. The sun is now well up in the sky, warm on your back as you walk away, leaving the Sea of Galilee and the crowds behind.

22

The Cure of the Paralytic –

Mark 2: 1–12

When he returned to Capernaum, some time later, word went round that he was in the house, and so many people collected that there was no room left, even in front of the door. He was preaching the word to them when some people came, bringing him a paralytic carried by four men, but as they could not get the man to him through the crowd, they stripped the roof over the place where Jesus was and when they had made an opening, they lowered the stretcher on which the paralytic lay. Seeing their faith, Jesus said to the paralytic, 'My child, your sins are forgiven.' Now some scribes were sitting there, and they thought to themselves, 'How can this man talk like that? He is being blasphemous. Who but God can forgive sins?' And at once, Jesus, inwardly aware that this is what they were thinking, said to them, 'Why do you have these thoughts in your hearts? Which of these is easier: to say to the paralytic, "Your sins are forgiven," or to say, "Get up, pick up your stretcher and walk"? But to prove to you that the Son of Man has authority to forgive sins on Earth...' – he said to the paralytic – 'I order you: Get up, pick up your stretcher, and go off home.' And the man got up, and at once picked up his stretcher and walked out in front of everyone, so that they were all astonished and praised God saying, 'We have never seen anything like this.'

The Cure of the Paralytic – Mark 2: 1–12

❖❖❖

Imagine that you and three others, friends and family, are together in a house in Capernaum.

The house is dark and cool. Before you, on the floor, lies a man on a light bed used as a stretcher to carry him around because he is paralysed.

He is a dear relative of yours and you have asked these other people to help you today.

This man has been paralysed for many years.

You know that Jesus has returned to Capernaum, and you have grown to love and trust this man from Galilee.

The decision had come quickly; this could be the last chance to help your relative. It's now or never; Jesus could leave at any time. The urge to see him is overpowering; you feel strongly that this is the right thing to do.

Together, the four of you place the carrying straps over your shoulders and lift the man off the floor and carry him out of the house into the sunlit street.

The street is strangely empty, save only for stray dogs, camels and donkeys tethered to their posts.

You can hear the murmur of people, a large crowd, and you make your way towards them; you know that this is where Jesus must be.

You turn the corner and there is the crowd; hundreds are standing near a house which is full of people.

You cannot see the door for people. You are close behind the crowd, but no one will let you through; they also want to see Jesus.

You feel desperately disappointed. Why didn't you come earlier? But you are determined not to be beaten.

You look up. The only empty space is on the flat roof. The roof is made of clay, but you know there is an area at the back which is only covered with palm leaves which is used to lower and raise items like bedding or food and drink.

You and your friends lift up the man and his bed and walk around the crowd to the rear of the house and climb the outside steps leading onto the flat roof.

This isn't easy; the two men at the back lift the bed up high and keep it level.

You are now on the roof, and you can see in the corner the palm leaves you are looking for.

You can hear Jesus talking below; the crowd is silent.

Your friends are shocked to see you remove the palms, but nothing is going to stop you now.

Deep down you know the man you can hear below is the answer to all your problems.

Jesus' voice is clearer now but you still can't see him.

You tell the others the man can be lowered into the room below; Jesus will see him and that will be enough.

The hole is just big enough and, using the carrying straps and by lying on your stomach, you can lower the stretcher to the floor below.

People in the room are forced to make space and there are many disgruntled people who resent the intrusion.

Jesus has stopped speaking. For a moment as you lie there you suddenly feel a little afraid – what have you done? You can see some scribes in the room – what will they have to say?

But your cares leave you when Jesus appears below and looks up. He smiles; he seems amused. Then he looks at the man at his feet. With great compassion he gently says to the man, 'My child, your sins are forgiven.'

After saying this, Jesus looks up at you, four faces peering down. You look into his eyes and you feel such gladness – yes, what you did was right, your faith in this man is fulfilled; he has cured your relative but you also feel cured.

But looking down you can see the man has not got off his bed. He looks uncertain. The scribes are unhappy; they are outraged to hear Jesus forgiving him his sins. Only God, they say, can forgive sins; Jesus is blaspheming.

The man is afraid to move and remains on the bed.

Jesus responds to the scribes and asks them why they have these thoughts in their hearts. He asks them, which is easier, do they think, to tell a man his sins are forgiven and cure the root of his problem, or to cure his physical illness and tell him to get up, pick up his stretcher and walk?

Then Jesus' demeanour changes; his kind, compassionate nature becomes one of cold authority. 'I order you,' he says to the paralytic. 'Pick up your stretcher and go off home.'

Your relative gives a quick look at the scribes, then quickly gets up and makes his way out through the crowds, carrying his bed.

You can see the scribes' faces; they have felt the divine authority of Jesus and feel diminished. They were not impressed with Jesus' compassion, now they have been silenced by his astounding authority.

Jesus had shown them that with his love he can forgive sins, but he also had divine power to cure physical illness.

You have watched everything, and now your relative is cured, you want to thank Jesus, but how can you put into words what you feel? Jesus looks up into your face. Your eyes meet. He smiles at you again; you smile back. There is no need for words.

23

Jesus Calms the Storm – Mark 4: 35-41

With the coming of the evening that same day, he said to them, 'Let us cross over to the other side.' And leaving the crowd behind they took him, just as he was, in the boat; and there were other boats with him. Then it began to blow a great gale and the waves were breaking into the boat so that it was almost swamped. But he was in the stern, his head on the cushion, asleep. They woke him and said to him, 'Master, do you not care? We are lost!' And he woke up and rebuked the wind and said to the sea, 'Quiet now! Be calm!' And the wind dropped, and there followed a great calm. Then he said to them, 'Why are you so frightened? Have you still no faith?' They were overcome with awe and said to one another, 'Who can this be? Even the wind and the sea obey him.'

❖❖❖

Jesus has been addressing hundreds of people all day. You have been listening to him. You have heard many parables, some familiar, having heard them many times before, but Jesus always had something new to say.

You feel tired and you know Jesus needs to get away from the crowds.

You are not surprised when he suggests that you and the rest of the disciples row him across the lake to the other side where he can rest and pray.

Even though you are tired, you also want to get away from the crowd and are prepared to row.

So you make your way to the boat with Jesus and help him aboard.

You are standing in the water, holding onto the side of the boat and watch Jesus as he makes his way to the stern. He sits down heavily on some cushions placed there for passengers.

You climb on-board, take your seat and your oar from the bottom of the boat and place it in the rowlock.

People are still standing on the shore; they can never hear enough from Jesus; they hate to see him leave.

But the boat pulls away and leaves them on the bank.

Hear the splash of the oars in the water, the creaking boat, the water slapping on the wooden sides.

You pull on the oars You hear the splash of blades and the creaking oars as the men pull on them.

Heavy clouds have shortened the day, night is quickly coming; there is no sunset.

You are facing the rear of the boat and can see Jesus. He has fallen asleep on the cushions.

You feel glad to have him safe on-board, he deserves some peace. It feels good to have his trust.

Jesus Calms the Storm – Mark 4: 35–41

You put your back into rowing. You have a special passenger; it is a joy to serve him and to know he trusts you.

A gust of wind rocks the boat as you reach the middle of the lake. The boat begins to heave as big waves crash into the sides.

Those dark clouds should have warned you; a sudden storm has rolled down from the mountain not uncommon for this lake. Why did you agree to this?

The wind gets stronger, and with it comes the rain. Soon you and the whole crew are soaked.

There is a flash of lightning; it shows the height of the waves and the white foaming tops. Another flash and in it you see Jesus, his head covered, still asleep.

In the darkness a loud rumble of thunder just above the boat.

The waves are growing bigger; the boat heaves, the bow up in the air, then plunging into the waves.

Water is coming over the sides; your feet are in water; your oar is useless; the boat is uncontrollable; you are at the mercy of the storm. Fear grips your heart.

You fear for Jesus' life more than your own.

Surely he must help, but another flash of lightning shows him still asleep.

Men are bailing water instead of rowing; shouts of alarm are drowned by the thunder.

The mast breaks with a loud crack and crashes down close to you.

You feel powerless against this angry storm.

You must wake Jesus – why has he not woken?

You leave your oar on the bottom of the boat and slowly make your way along the heaving deck and come close to Jesus. He still sleeps; his hood covers his head. In spite of the rain, the storm, the awful danger, he sleeps like a child.

You must wake him; he is your only hope, the only one who can save your life. You touch his shoulder, you shake it. Jesus wakes up and looks up at you.

'Master, how can you sleep through this storm? We are sinking; we are going to drown.'

Jesus stands up; he has seen the fear in your eyes. He shouts back at the storm; you hear his voice above the thunder. He addresses the wind and the sea as if they were his kindred, 'Quiet now, be calm.'

And the wind drops as suddenly as it came, waves stop pounding the boat and soon all is quiet, the boat gently rocking, only the sound of water swilling in the bottom of the boat.

All the disciples behind you are exhausted and are looking in awe at Jesus. He asks, 'Why were you so frightened? How is it that you have no faith?'

You understand. You had all fought the storm and nearly drowned; you had only to ask Jesus and he would have saved you.

You and the disciples tonight have discovered how great your leader is. While in danger and great fear, you called on Jesus, and you discovered his power to save.

You hear the disciples murmuring, 'Who can this man be? Even the wind and the sea obey him.'

You go back to your seat and take up your oar. The first light of dawn appears over the mountains; the same mountains that gave you the storm now herald a new day.

Through distress you have found your Saviour.

24

The Gerasene Demoniac –
Mark 5: 1–20

They reached the territory of the Gerasenes on the other side of the lake, and when he disembarked, a man with an unclean spirit at once came out from the tombs towards him. The man lived in the tombs and no one could secure him any more, even with a chain, because he had often been secured with fetters and chains but had snapped the chains and broken the fetters, and no one had the strength to control him. All night and all day, among the tombs and in the mountains, he would howl and gash himself with stones. Catching sight of Jesus from a distance, he ran up and fell at his feet and shouted at the top of his voice, 'What do you want with me, Jesus, Son of the Most High God? In God's name do not torture me!' For Jesus had been saying to him, 'Come out of the man, unclean spirit.' Then he asked, 'What is your name?' He answered, 'My name is Legion, for there are many of us.' And he begged him earnestly not to send them out of the district. Now on the mountainside there was a great herd of pigs feeding, and the unclean spirits begged him, 'Send us to the pigs; let us go into them.' So he gave them leave. With that, the unclean spirits came out and went into the pigs, and the herd of about two thousand pigs charged down the cliff into the lake, and there they were drowned. The men looking after them ran off and told their story in the city and in the country round about, and the people came to see what had really happened. They came to Jesus and saw the demoniac sitting there – the man who had had the legion in him – properly dressed and in his full senses, and they were afraid. And those who had witnessed it reported what had happened to the demoniac and what had become of the pigs. Then they began to implore Jesus to leave their neighbourhood. As he was getting into the boat, the man who had been possessed begged to be allowed to stay with him. Jesus would not let him but said to him, 'Go home to your people and tell them all that the Lord in His mercy has done for you.' So the man went off and proceeded to proclaim in the Decapolis all that Jesus had done for him. And everyone was amazed.

❖❖❖

Be aware of the thoughts and feelings the story evokes in you.

Jesus and the disciples are getting out of a boat. They are still shaken by the fright they had during the storm and the amazing powers of Jesus. See that boat, the ropes being tied to the wooden landing at the lakeside.

The air is still now, just the sound of gently lapping water against the side of the boat. Gulls are circling above; see how white they are against the clear blue sky.

Watch now as Jesus gets out of the boat. He steps onto the grassy shore. The disciples finish tying up the boat and follow Jesus as he climbs up away from the lake. You see other people are there and they walk along with them.

Above, you can see a large graveyard, full of big stone tombs; these graves extend high up the hillside, all shapes and sizes.

The Gerasene Demoniac – Mark 5: 1–20

Suddenly the air is filled with a loud cry, a tormented yell, quite alarming and strange. It's coming from the graveyard.

The screaming continues, loud, hostile, fierce, threatening – what kind of human being could make such an unearthly noise?

Your instinct is to move on as quickly as you can from this haunting, disturbing sound.

The locals tell you that it's the voice of a well-known insane, possessed mad-man. Best to ignore him; leave him up there where he lives among the tombs. They have tried for many years to help him but now he is completely out of control; chains can't hold him. He's dangerous; no one can talk to him any more; he's a menace to society; he howls all night and cuts himself.

The local people are embarrassed and try to hurry Jesus onward towards the village.

The disciples feel protective towards Jesus and also want to move on.

But suddenly the worst happens: the screaming madman appears from the tombs close to Jesus.

You look at the man; he is half naked, his clothes torn and filthy, his body covered in dirt, a long matted beard down to his chest. See his feet and legs, cut and bleeding.

You look at his face: wild staring eyes, hostile suspicious eyes look at Jesus half hidden by long matted hair. What colour are his eyes? Now you see something else; there is sadness and a longing in them. He is a lonely man, a complete outcast; he has no friends or family. A lost soul, living rough in the cold shelter of the deserted tombs. He can only live off the scraps he can steal from people who hate and fear him.

He is approaching Jesus. You watch to see how Jesus will handle his encounter with this wild, unpredictable man. What will he say? What will he do?

The man falls at Jesus' feet. He speaks to Jesus. 'What,' he asks, 'do you want from me, Son of God? Will you reject and torment me like all the rest?'

Jesus is calm; you can see only compassion in his face. He reaches out and puts his hand gently on the man's shoulder and looks into his eyes and quietly asks the man, 'Who are you? What is your name?'

'I am many people; I don't know who I am. Can you tell me? Can you give me back my self, my identity, which I lost long ago? My mind is tormented; free me from my demons.'

Jesus continues to look calmly and lovingly into the man's eyes.

You see a change in the man's face; his eyes are calmer, his face no longer contorted, savage or fearful. He has experienced Jesus' total acceptance of him as a human being; he feels accepted, forgiven, even loved for the first time in his life.

The man grasps Jesus' hand as it rests on his shoulder; he kisses it several times and tears run down his cheeks. He still holds Jesus' hand and looks into Jesus' eyes. Now his eyes are calm; a stillness comes over him, a profound peace fills his whole being. He looks in wonder and gratitude as Jesus raises him to his feet. They embrace. Jesus turns away and leaves the man standing. He has found himself again, he can love again, and he knows he loves this man, Jesus. He is now at peace with himself and others; he is able to care for himself now.

You have seen Jesus calm a frightening storm, now you have seen him calm the storm that can enrage and destroy people's minds.

You go up to the man as he stands there and you take your coat off and place it on his shoulders. He looks at you and says, 'Thank you.'

25

Cure of a Blind Man at Bethsaida - Mark 8: 14-21

They came to Bethsaida, and some people brought to him a blind man whom they begged him to touch. He took the blind man by the hand and led him outside the village. Then putting spittle on his eyes and laying his hands on him, he asked, 'Can you see anything?' The man, who was beginning to see, replied, 'I can see people; they look like trees to me, but they are walking about.' Then he laid his hands on the man's eyes again and he saw clearly; he was cured, and he could see everything plainly and distinctly. And Jesus sent him home, saying, 'Do not even go into the village.'

❖❖❖

Imagine that you are a married man, with a wife and children. Since you lost your sight your family have been reduced to begging on the streets.

You are still fit and strong but unable to work, being totally dependant on your family for all your needs.

Cure of a Blind Man at Bethsaida - Mark 8: 14–21

Being once a happy fulfilled husband and father, respected by all as an honest workman, you are now depressed and rendered helpless through blindness and have little hope for the future.

Your wife and children are all persuading you to go with them into the village nearby where there is a man who has cured many with the touch of his hand.

Your wife has great faith in this man they call Jesus and the children join her in persuading you to leave the house.

The smallest child has taken your hand and is trying to pull you to your feet.

Feel the little hand as it grips your fingers as you reluctantly rise from the chair and find your walking stick close by.

As you stand, there is total blackness before you, you cannot see the bright sunlight which you know fills the doorway.

The door that leads into your garden where now your wife, her hand on your arm, leads you into the sunshine.

You feel its warmth but see only blackness.

Your stick taps the baked earth; you can remember the vegetables you used to grow and which are now scarce, tended only by the children.

It is good to feel the sun on your face and the light breeze. You can smell the grass and flowering trees but they only serve to remind you of the days when your role had been so different as head of family and respected workman.

The family still love you and you are touched by their concern but your depression is not lifted and you only venture out to please them.

So you walk along with the children; you can hear them skipping and talking excitedly; you long to share their hope in a cure for your blindness.

Your wife holds your arm but is strangely quiet.

You are now entering the village; new sounds are coming from a distant crowd of people. One voice can be heard over the rest; it must be the voice of Jesus who your wife has spoken about.

She has spoken with loving respect about this man's words and actions. She has told you that his words have given her strength to carry on since your blindness changed everything.

She wants to take you to him, she says his touch can heal you. To please her you and the family approach Jesus who you are told is sitting under a tree having finished his teaching.

The children have become quiet and you can feel them close to you, some holding onto your clothes; the smallest is hiding behind your legs.

Your wife's hand is trembling as it rests on your arm.

A longing is now awakened within you, not just for your sake but for your family, and you dearly want to be cured.

You are leaving the crowd behind and you begin to sense the closeness of Jesus.

With a firm grip on your arm your wife leads you towards him, and the children follow.

Your wife speaks and you hear her respectfully but earnestly ask Jesus to touch you so that your blindness can be cured.

The older children join her, pleading in their childish way which you try to control.

Jesus doesn't speak but you sense that he is listening.

Cure of a Blind Man at Bethsaida - Mark 8: 14-21

As your wife quietens the children you know she is pleased to have this chance to present you to this man in whom she has such great trust.

Even though you cannot see Jesus a stillness has fallen upon you, you are unafraid and have forgotten for a moment your desire for a cure.

A profound sense of wellbeing has overwhelmed all desire, you are only conscious of the present.

Your wife has released your arm and you stand alone; the children remain quiet, all you hear is the distant murmuring crowd, you have a deep sense of peace.

You are content to stand and wait until your hand is gently but firmly taken. It could be the hand of a fellow workman, you can feel its strength, its calloused skin.

You are being led away by Jesus and you follow unresistingly.

Your family are left behind; you can hear Jesus' footsteps beside you as you leave the village and enter the fields.

Now under your feet you feel the grass and hear the rattle of sheep bells and birdsong in the trees.

Jesus has stopped and in peaceful silence you wait, not knowing what is going to happen.

A serenity has overwhelmed you; time doesn't exist in his presence and all desire has gone. You are content and ready to accept anything. This encounter with Jesus transcends everything.

Now you feel moist fingers touch your closed eyes, hands are placed on your head and you are having the blessing of Jesus.

In your stillness light breaks into your darkness, and as your eyes slowly open, bright sunlight floods your whole being.

Dark shapes are moving in the distance; are they trees or people?

Now you see the face of Jesus and your eyes meet.

He asks in a quiet voice, 'Can you see anything?'

You try to explain to him but in your excitement you say, 'I can see people; they look like trees to me, but they are walking about.'

He understands your difficulty and as he places his hands over your eyes the darkness returns, but when they are removed your sight is clear.

You can see people at the edge of the village and also your family watching intently.

You long to share your joy with them but as you grasp Jesus' hand and kiss it in gratitude he instructs you not to return to the village.

You don't understand but so complete is your trust in him that you immediately begin to make your way home.

Your private time with Jesus is over but will never be forgotten.

Not only can you see again but you have glimpsed and felt the sublime.

Jesus has given you a new life which you are ready to share with your family who you know will be waiting.

26

The Blind Man of Jericho – Mark 10: 46–52

They reached Jericho; and as he left Jericho with his disciples and a large crowd, Bartimaeus (that is the son of Timaus), a blind beggar, was sitting at the side of the road. When he heard that it was Jesus of Nazareth, he began to shout and to say, 'Son of David, Jesus, have pity on me.' And many of them scolded him and told him to keep quiet, but he only shouted all the louder, 'Son of David, have pity on me.' Jesus stopped and said, 'Call him here.' So they called the blind man. 'Courage,' they said, 'get up; he is calling you.' So throwing off his cloak, he jumped up and went to Jesus. Then Jesus spoke, 'What do you want me to do for you?' 'Rabbuni,' the blind man said to him, 'Master, let me see again.' Jesus said to him, 'Go; your faith has saved you.' And immediately his sight returned and he followed him along the road.

❖❖❖

Jesus is leaving Jericho with his disciples, and a large crowd of followers; among them is Zacchaeus the once rich tax collector still full of gratitude for the new life he has received from Jesus.

We can never experience complete blindness just by closing our eyes but try and become such a person who might sit at the gate of Jericho relying on the compassion of others for your food and water. Some may give you money or old clothes. All day you sit and when evening comes you make your way to a friend's house to sleep.

Blindness struck as you reached adulthood, leaving you totally dependant on others.

Another day has arrived and here you sit by the gate wall where you will be seen by people entering and leaving Jericho.

The sun has darkened your skin, your brown hands outstretched as you beg with a voice softened with constant pleading.

Everyone knows your name and you must keep on good terms with traders and shoppers depending as you do on their charity.

Today there seem to be more people than usual but you are receiving less attention. The people are animated and you feel expectancy in the excited crowd as they gather along the road.

The crowd is dense; you can no longer feel the sun; you are ignored and you beg louder trying to be heard above the chatter but no one hears.

A young lad who often keeps you company tells you that Jesus of Nazareth is leaving Jericho and will soon be coming through the gate.

You have heard many people speak of this man, how he has cured the sick and brought hope to many.

The excitement is increasing, people's feet are very close; afraid of being trampled on, you wave your stick as a warning.

Now the crowd becomes quiet, only a few cry out; you ask the lad what is happening and he tells you that Jesus is passing by.

The Blind Man of Jericho - Mark 10: 46–52

You remain hidden by the crowd and listen to their soft supplications; the people call blessings on his name and are honouring him with their respect and gratitude.

Hope of regaining your sight was buried many years ago, but your spirit is awakened; this man has great power and compassion; you must reach out to him, you may never get another chance.

Your voice, normally subdued and pleading, becomes full and loud and you shout, 'Son of God, Jesus, have pity one me.'

Your voice rises over the crowd and echoes on the gate walls.

People are shocked to hear you cry out hidden and forgotten behind them; they try to silence you and impatiently tell you to keep quiet.

In their eyes you are not worthy to encounter Jesus. Your audacity is embarrassing.

But the spirit is strong within you and at the risk of losing their goodwill you shout out into your darkness, 'Son of David, have pity on me.'

There is silence, the sound of feet on the road has stopped.

You hear a single clear voice, 'Call him here.'

Who is being called? The lad tells you that Jesus is asking for you and the people near you are helping you to your feet and encouraging you to move forward.

With a new strength in your body you throw off the impeding cloak and with the lad guiding you through the crowd you are led along the road to Jesus.

You see nothing but feel a stillness come upon you and know that you are in his presence.

You are glad but also fearful of the change this encounter will make to your life.

You hear him speak; the nearness of his voice surprises but also consoles you. 'What do you want me to do for you?'

For years you have only asked for alms, now you can ask for your deepest longing.

'Rabbuni, let me see again.'

All your life you believed that your blindness was punishment from God, either for your sins or your father's. You can believe Jesus has the power to reverse that sentence and allow you to see again.

You don't know where your faith springs from; it feels new but you feel that you have known this man all your life.

Your encounter is brief and he tells you, 'Go; your faith has saved you.'

Light bursts painfully into your eyes and you can see again. You look into the eyes of the man before you and you know he has given you more than sight but forgiveness and fulfilment that is yours forever.

Jesus moves away and his disciples follow. You are also free to follow, leaving your begging place and cloak behind. Wherever this man goes you want to be with him.

You only have the worn clothing you stand in, but you have found your heart's longing which feels even greater than the gift of sight.

The man walking beside you tells you his name is Zacchaeus and wants you to accept some money.

27

Jesus and the Little Children –

Mark 10: 13–16

People were bringing little children to him, for him to touch them. The disciples scolded them, but when Jesus saw this he was indignant and said to them, 'Let the little children come to me; do not stop them; for it is to such as these that the kingdom of God belongs. In truth I tell you, anyone who does not welcome the kingdom of God like a little child will never enter it.' Then he embraced them, laid his hands on them and gave them his blessing.

❖❖❖

Can you imagine being one of those children in the Gospel scene?

Your parents have taken you out for the day; they are holding your hands and are leading you along the road towards a crowd of people.

Can you feel your hands in theirs? Your mother's hand is soft and smooth, your father's feels bigger, harder – the skin is rougher.

You are out in the country; the crowd of people are gathered near a large tree.

As you get nearer you can hear a man's voice, clear as a bell over the heads of the strangely quiet crowd.

Your parents are now taking you through the crowd who let you pass to the front.

Now you can see where the voice was coming from. Under the tree sits a man alone. A strong looking man who must be very important, having the attention of so many people.

You are feeling a little shy being in the front, so close to this man, but there are other children close to you, and you hold on tight to your parents' hands.

You whisper, 'Who is this man?' and you are told that he helped many people in many different ways, he is Jesus of Nazareth.

Jesus has finished speaking to the people and this is the moment for all the parents with their children to move forward and get nearer to Jesus and ask for his blessing.

Your parents move forward and as you get near to him the men who were behind Jesus step forward and hold up their hands to stop you getting any closer. 'No don't come any closer, get back into the crowd,' they say.

Your parents stop and you look at Jesus; what will he say?

You hear again the clear warm tones of Jesus' voice, 'Let the children come to me; do not stop them; for it is to such as these that the kingdom of God belongs.'

Your parents are relieved and animated, yes this man is indeed special; you have lost any fear you may have had, and let go of your parents' hands and run up to Jesus and stand by his knee.

Jesus looks at you and immediately puts his arm around your shoulders and gently sits you on his knee.

Jesus and the Little Children - Mark 10: 13–16

You have no fear; this great man is smiling at you; you dare to look into his eyes. You feel loved, treasured, you are more important in his eyes than anything else in the world.

You are just a child, not important in the world's eyes, you have nothing to tell Jesus that will impress him, what use are you to him? Why should he be interested in you?

You look closer into his eyes; what does it matter? You feel loved, accepted and safe, and that is more than enough. You smile back at him and he hugs you even closer, you have given him what he wants, your love and your trust.

His voice is close now as he speaks to the men behind, 'I tell you solemnly, anyone who does not welcome the kingdom of God like a little child will never enter it.'

He places his hands on your head and gives you his blessing. Feel his hands on your head as he speaks your name. You will always cherish this moment, and it will be a source of strength throughout your life.

A profound peace remains with you as Jesus gently lifts you off his knee and you return to your parents.

Childhood memories can be a strong influence in our lives, some good, some bad; the good ones are often the simplest moments which nonetheless make a deep and lasting impression.

Now we are grown up, how have our prayers changed? What voices now tell you that you are not important enough to get close to Jesus, that you don't deserve to be loved or, what have you done to deserve his blessing?

The child on Jesus' knee had no gifts and had no requests; your exchange of love was enough; you felt Jesus' love for you and you gave him your love in return; no need for words, this was the key to his heart and the key into his kingdom.

28

Miracle of the Loaves –
Luke 9: 12–17

It was late afternoon when the twelve came up to him and said, 'Send the people away, and they can go to the villages and farms round about to find lodging and food; for we are in a lonely place here.' He replied, 'Give them something to eat yourselves.' But they said, 'We have no more than five loaves and two fish, unless we are to go ourselves and buy food for all these people.' For there were about five thousand men. But he said to his disciples, 'Get them to sit down in parties of about fifty.' They did so and made them all sit down. Then he took the five loaves and the two fish, raised his eyes to heaven, and said the blessing over them; then he broke them and handed them to his disciples to distribute among the crowd. They all ate as much as they wanted, and when the scraps left over were collected they filled twelve baskets.

❖❖❖

You are a disciple of Jesus, and with the others had obeyed him and entered the villages and towns and had spoken to people about the new kingdom which Jesus was proclaiming. A new kingdom that fulfilled the ancient laws of Judaism. The people had listened to you and many had responded. You had been able also to heal people, and had achieved things you know were beyond your power. It had all been a gift from God.

You have all shared these experiences with Jesus and your gratitude to him is beyond measure. Now he suggests that today would be a good time to rest and recuperate. You always welcomed these periods when you had Jesus to yourselves and he would talk to you about the new kingdom and teach you how to pray.

You all walk with him into the hills not far from the town of Bethsaida. The day has been hot; the earth is dry and dusty as you walk along. You reach a hill higher than the others and you all sit on its grassy slope, and you look down on the town below. The air is beginning to cool and a slight breeze is on your face. Smell the fresh air; you feel at peace.

You have all you need, your companions are near and Jesus the beloved is close at hand. A deep feeling of satisfaction adds to your contentment; your mission has been successful; Jesus, you know, is pleased with you.

You have nothing to show for your success, not as when you had sold a good catch of fish. This was different: your reward had been to see people's faces change from sadness to joy. Now more people knew about Jesus and his new kingdom.

Your contentment is disturbed; coming up the hillside you can see crowds of people coming in search of Jesus. There is no escape; more is being asked of you. You know Jesus will receive them in his usual compassionate way.

You are surprised at the numbers: there must be hundreds, maybe thousands, too many to count. Men, women, children, the old, the crippled. When they all stop as near to Jesus as they can, Jesus welcomes them and addresses them by telling them again about the good news, that they are all loved and forgiven children of God.

You watch as many are healed by Jesus. The crowd is animated; cries of gratitude and thanks come in abundance.

It's now late afternoon; the sun is low in the sky; it will soon be dark. You feel hungry as do the other disciples. You realise that no one on the hillside has eaten all day.

You approach Jesus. You take the initiative and suggest that it's time to let these people go home so that they can get something to eat. When they are gone, you will be free to eat the food which you brought with you.

You are taken aback when Jesus says, 'Why don't you share your food with these people?'

Is he serious? How can five loaves and two fishes feed thousands? Perhaps you could go into the town and buy some food.

But no, Jesus tells you to get the people to sit on the grass in groups of fifty.

You are now among the happy throng and they gladly sit down. This is not what they had expected; they thought the time to go home had come – what more had Jesus to say to them?

You return to Jesus; you are carrying the precious food. You take the basket from off your shoulder and open it up. You take out five loaves, feel their crusty surface. The smell of fresh bread increases your appetite. You place each one on the ground before Jesus. You put your hand into the basket again and take out two large fish, cooked and wrapped in a cloth. You place them with the loaves.

You watch Jesus take a loaf and a fish into his hands; he looks up to heaven and says, 'Blessed are you, Father of all creation;

we have this food to eat, fruit of the earth and the work of men's hands.' Then he breaks the bread and divides the fish.

Jesus looks at you. He asks for your basket; he fills it with loaves and fish. You leave him and go among the crowd, giving the people equal amounts of food. What are your thoughts? You can only satisfy a few, not all. You begin to feel a bit foolish.

But you realise you are not the only one giving out food. You can see all the other disciples are feeding the crowd.

Jesus somehow has filled their baskets as well. Where did all this food come from?

Your success out in the country districts had amazed you, but now this experience of working with Jesus has left you speechless.

Does the crowd realise what has happened? They are delighted to be fed. You know that there is a deep mystery behind this simple example of Jesus' compassion for everyone. He cares for their physical needs as well as their spiritual needs.

The day is over, night has come. The people begin to go home. Now you can see on the ground the flattened grass where people sat, and scraps of food; they had had more than enough. You begin to tidy the place up, putting the scraps into your basket. It becomes full and when you get back to Jesus the other disciples have also filled theirs as well with leftover food.

The generosity of God is so abundant, beyond that which anyone could imagine.

29

Jesus Walks on Water and, With Him, Peter – Matthew 14: 22-33

And at once he made the disciples get into the boat and go on ahead to the other side while he sent the crowds away. After sending the crowds away, he went up into the hills by himself to pray. When evening came, he was there alone, while the boat, by now some furlongs from the land, was hard pressed by rough waves, for there was a headwind. In the fourth watch of the night he came towards them, walking on the sea, and when the disciples saw him walking on the sea they were terrified. 'It is a ghost,' they said, and cried out in fear. But at once Jesus called out to them, saying, 'Courage! It's me! Don't be afraid.' It was Peter who answered. 'Lord,' he said, 'if it is you, tell me to come to you across the water.' Jesus said, 'Come.' Then Peter got out of the boat and started walking towards Jesus across the water, but then, noticing the wind, he took fright and began to sink. 'Lord,' he cried, 'save me!' Jesus put out his hand at once and held him. 'You have so little faith,' he said, 'why did you doubt?' And as they got into the boat the wind dropped. The men in the boat bowed down before him and said, 'Truly, you are the Son of God.'

❖ ❖ ❖

Jesus Walks on Water and, With Him, Peter – Matthew 14: 22–33

Today you have been with Jesus among the hills near the Sea of Galilee. Thousands of people have also been with you. With his help you achieved what you had thought impossible. With rations barely enough for yourselves, you and the disciples have fed everyone on the lake shore.

Now the day is over, all the followers of Jesus have been fed, and Jesus has spoken to them for the last time; they all agree to leave him in peace and return to their homes.

You are now all alone with Jesus and night is descending. The crowds have gone; the boat is waiting to depart. Jesus tells you to take the boat and leave him on this side of the lake. You're not comfortable with leaving him alone but you know how much he needs to pray.

You all say goodbye to him, and you, with the others, take your place in the boat. Hear the familiar sounds: water lapping the sides of the boat, the rattle of oars being placed in the rowlocks. Peter always gives the order to row. You pull on your oar.

Can you feel the smooth wooden oar in your hands, the hard seat beneath you, your feet pushing against the foot rest in front? See the back of the disciple in front as he leans forward to pull on his oar.

You look back at the shore and you can see Jesus alone in the fading light as he climbs up the hillside. It is strange to see him alone, no other person in sight. You respect his need for solitude.

Now it is completely dark; you can't see the shore any more. The waves now drum loudly on the side of the boat. Sudden storms are common on this huge freshwater lake. The strong wind is blowing spray into your face but you must keep rowing through the hissing waves. You hear Peter's voice above the storm, urging you on.

The storm continues, the boat heaves and rolls. Your oar is out of the water; it's hard to control the boat.

Peter's voice is no longer part of the storm urging you on – why has he become silent? You look back and see him holding the rudder. He looks like a statue; his eyes are transfixed; he is staring incredulously out into the storm ahead of the boat.

Peter doesn't speak, he just points out into the storm. You turn to look where he is pointing, and you can't believe your eyes: there is a figure walking on the waves. You shake the shoulder of the man in front and point at the figure.

All the men are alarmed; they also have seen it; it can only be a ghost. You are terrified – what dreadful omen of the storm is this?

But the apparition shouts out and at once you recognise the voice of Jesus, 'Have courage, men, I am here, don't be alarmed.'

The noise of the storm seems to abate, the waves not so high, the boat rises and falls on gentler waves.

You hear Peter speak loud and clear, 'Lord, if it is you, tell me to come to you across the water.'

Peter always wanted to share in everything Jesus did; you all wanted to be closely involved with Jesus but no one more than Peter.

Jesus responds to Peter and invites him to come to him.

You hold on tight to your oar and hold your breath. Peter is getting out over the side of the boat; he will drown. But he doesn't sink, and you watch him move away from the boat. He is also walking on the surface of the water, moving towards Jesus.

Peter is rising and falling with the waves. There is still a wind, and a sudden gust tears at his cloak. He takes his eyes off Jesus

Jesus Walks on Water and, With Him, Peter – Matthew 14: 22–33

and looks at the waves around him; his arms go up and with a cry he sinks into the lake, 'Lord save me!' Jesus is near and is lifting him up out of the water and together they come to the boat.

When safe on-board Jesus puts his hand on Peter's shoulder and says to him, 'Man of little faith, why did you doubt?'

You look at the two men. You know Jesus has called you and you have followed him, but often you feel afraid; like Peter you can move forward but when you sense new ground, the unfamiliar, you hold back – any change is frightening: keep to the familiar, retreat from the new. Tonight you realise that to be able to continue your life's journey, you must keep your eyes on Jesus. Only he can save you.

30

The Adulterous Woman –

John 8: 1–11

Jesus went to the Mount of Olives. At daybreak he appeared in the temple again, and as all the people came to him, he sat down and began to teach them. The scribes and Pharisees brought a woman who had been caught committing adultery, and making her stand there in the middle they said to Jesus, 'Master, this woman was caught in the very act of committing adultery, and the Law of Moses has ordered us to stone women of this kind. What have you got to say?' They asked him this as a test, looking for an accusation to use against him. But Jesus bent down and started writing on the ground with his finger. As they persisted with their question, he straightened up and said, 'Let the one among you who is guiltless be the first to throw a stone at her.' Then he bent down and continued writing on the ground. When they heard this they went away one by one, beginning with the eldest, until the last one had gone and Jesus was left alone with the woman, who remained in the middle. Jesus again straightened up and said, 'Woman, where are they? Has no one condemned you?' 'No one, sir,' she replied. 'Neither do I condemn you,' said Jesus. 'Go away, and from this moment sin no more.'

❖ ❖ ❖

The Adulterous Woman – John 8: 1–11

Imagine that you are sitting on a wall inside the Temple in Jerusalem. You are looking down on the dusty courtyard near the main gate.

You know that this is where Jesus often speaks to the crowds; you know that there will be many people there later all wanting to listen to his words.

You were up early, Jesus starts his day early, and now here you are sitting on a wall inside the Temple. The sky is beginning to change, a golden light is touching the high towers of the Temple; you begin to feel the warmth of the sun on your back. The cold night soon changes into soft warmth by the early morning sun. You know that this is the moment Jesus appears, he will soon be here, just below you, in the dusty courtyard.

But now the place is quiet, only the soft fluttering of doves' wings echo round the temple walls; hear their gentle clatter.

You enjoy this moment alone, the anticipation, the expectancy of seeing him. You know he will come.

Feel again the sun warm on your back, the hard rough stone against your legs.

Now as you watch, the yard below is quickly filling up with people: men, women and children. Some carry doves to make sacrifice.

One voice stands out above the rest and the crowd fall silent.

You had not noticed Jesus among the crowd until you heard the clear, familiar voice.

You are glad to see him again; he always gives you such comfort and hope, but also challenges that make you think.

You listen to him speak; his tone of voice is enough to give you the reassurance you long for.

Your attention is taken by a group of Pharisees who are pushing a woman through the crowd and place her to stand in front of Jesus.

Jesus stops talking; the crowd is murmuring, not sure what is happening.

One of the Pharisees speaks; in a loud voice so that all can hear, he addresses Jesus.

'Master, this woman was caught in the very act of adultery, and Moses has ordered us in the law to condemn women like this to death by stoning. What have you to say?'

You feel the tension in the crowd; the peace created by Jesus' voice is shattered, and the disturbing challenge affects everyone.

Look at this woman, she is on her way to execution. See her terrified face as she stands alone before Jesus. The crowd have moved back to distance themselves from this sinner.

Silence has fallen on the yard as all wait for Jesus' response.

In this silence all eyes including your own watch Jesus bend on one knee and start to write in the dust with his finger.

What can he be writing? Or is he drawing something?

The Pharisees look uneasy at this unexpected behaviour.

They ask again, 'What do you say, Master? Where does this woman stand in your kingdom that you speak of?'

Jesus quickly looks up, then stands before the crowd. The Pharisees are silent.

You are able to see Jesus' eyes as he speaks, see the compassion and love in them as he looks at the woman before him.

His reply opens up a new world, a world of different values.

His voice rings out loud and clear, 'If there is one of you who has not sinned, let him be the first to throw a stone at her.'

The Pharisees look at each other; none know how to respond to these words.

Jesus has transformed the whole scene. These same men who were about to carry out sentence on a woman guilty beyond doubt and on her way to execution under the law are now powerless to carry out the sentence.

No one speaks; neither you nor anyone else had ever thought about such things.

In a few words Jesus has made everyone aware of their own faults and need for forgiveness, and at the same time kindled compassion for a sinner and dispelled any thoughts of punishment.

There is no sound from the Pharisees, what answer can they give? No one is brave enough to confess that Jesus' words are true and humbling.

Watch as the speechless crowd moves away one by one. The oldest move first; the woman stands alone before Jesus; the yard is quiet, again all you can hear is the soft fluttering of wings.

Now you see Jesus again on one knee writing in the dust. The woman is watching him. He looks up. 'Woman, where are they? Has no one condemned you?'

See her frightened tearstained face; the soft morning breeze gently moves the strands of hair that hid her face. You hear the woman speak for the first time; her tearful eyes meet the compassionate eyes of Jesus.

'No one, sir,' she replies.

'Neither do I condemn you; go away and from this moment sin no more.'

Her face lights up; the most incredible thing has happened; she is filled with relief and gladness.

Her love and gratitude shows clearly in her eyes as she looks at Jesus.

You alone watch the two figures, Jesus and a loved forgiven sinner.

She slowly turns away and walks beneath you towards the temple gate. She walks a lonely road; how will her family and neighbours receive her? She has the inner strength, knowing that she has been forgiven, completely and finally, by the man she knows to be the Son of God.

Jesus stands alone. He looks up and sees you sitting on the wall. Your eyes meet.

31

The Transfiguration – Luke 9: 28-36

Now about eight days after this had been said, he took with him Peter, John and James and went up the mountain to pray. And it happened that, as he was praying, the aspect of his face was changed and his clothing became sparkling white. And suddenly there were two men talking to him; they were Moses and Elijah appearing in glory, and they were speaking of his passing which he was to accomplish in Jerusalem. Peter and his companions were heavy with sleep, but they woke and saw his glory and the two men standing with him. As these were leaving him, Peter said to Jesus, 'Master, it is wonderful for us to be here, so let us make three shelters, one for you, one for Moses and one for Elijah.' He did not know what he was saying. As he was saying this, a cloud came and covered them with shadow; and when they went into the cloud the disciples were afraid. And a voice came from the cloud saying, 'This is my Son, the Chosen One. Listen to him.' And after the voice had spoken, Jesus was found alone. The disciples kept silent and, at that time, told no one what they had seen.

❖❖❖

Imagine you are one of Jesus' disciples.

A few days ago he confronted you by asking who you thought he was.

Now he has invited you to go with him and climb Mount Tabor.

You know he likes to visit lonely quiet places where he prays to his Father, and always encourages you to do the same.

You are delighted and gladly go with him.

You are now climbing this rather steep hill.

It's a hot day. Feel the sun on your back. As you walk up the hill see the gorse bushes, the yellow flowers; smell their heavy scent in the warm air. You are careful on the stony path.

Jesus is leading; he seems to know the way.

You arrive at the top of the hill. The air is cooler. You enjoy the view below you.

Jesus suggests you sit down. He goes further, on his own, to pray.

It feels good to sit. Feel the grass with your hand.

A cool breeze on your face.

You close your eyes. Hear the bees in the gorse, a lark high in the sky above you. You begin to feel drowsy. The breeze is gentle, the sun warm.

You are conscious of Jesus still at prayer nearby.

You are surprised to hear voices and look towards Jesus.

He is standing with two men. You know instinctively that they are Moses and Elijah.

The Transfiguration – Luke 9: 28–36

But your attention is focused on Jesus. He looks different: his face seems to shine; his whole body is filled with light; his clothes a brilliant white. You are totally absorbed with Jesus. You hear a gentle voice saying, 'This is my Son, the Chosen One. Listen to him.'

You are filled with a sense of great peace. You feel safe; all your doubts and worries and regrets are gone. All you feel is peace and gladness. You belong, feel at home and have a part in Jesus' prayers, and you are in the presence of God, your Father.

Everyone is enfolded in a mist, full of light.

But in the middle of this heaven, you realise the two men are talking of Jesus' death, which is to happen in Jerusalem.

Why does this have to happen? Surely Jesus has the power to choose a different way.

Slowly the mist clears, the two men have gone, you are aware again of the boulders, the bushes, the view far below.

Peter doesn't want to leave. He wants to make a structure that will always be there as a memorial of such a moving experience.

But Jesus, deep in thought, signals that it's time to find the path which will take you back to the village below.

Psalm 84

How I love Your palace, Yahweh Sabaoth.
How my soul yearns and pines for Yahweh's courts.
My heart and my flesh sing for joy to the living God.
The sparrow has found its home at last.
The swallow a rest for its young, your altars
Yahweh Sabaoth my king and my God.
A single day in Your courts

Is worth more than a thousand elsewhere
Merely to stand on the steps of God's house
Is better than living with the wicked.
Yahweh Sabaoth, happy the man who
Puts his trust in You.

32

The Epileptic Demoniac – Luke 9: 37-43

Now on the following day when they were coming down from the mountain a large crowd came to meet him. Suddenly a man in the crowd cried out. 'Master,' he said, 'I implore you to look at my son; he is my only child. All at once a spirit will take hold of him, and give a sudden cry and throw the boy into convulsions with foaming at the mouth; it is slow to leave him, but when it does it leaves the boy worn out. I begged your disciples to cast it out, and they could not.' 'Faithless and perverse generation!' Jesus said in reply. 'How much longer must I be among you and put up with you? Bring your son here.' The boy was still moving towards Jesus when the devil threw him to the ground in convulsions. But Jesus rebuked the unclean spirit and cured the boy and gave him back to his father, and everyone was awestruck by the greatness of God.

❖❖❖

You and the other disciples are still silent as you descend from Mount Tabor.

You have experienced the presence of God when Jesus shared with you his own intimacy with his beloved Father.

Within that bright cloud on the hill top, you have felt raised from the earth and all its strife and suffering. With Jesus you had shared the serenity of God's love.

Now with considerable reluctance you are descending to live once more in the conflicts and challenges of life.

You have now left the hill behind but stop to look back once more at the hill top.

There is no mist and you can see the rocks that make the summit, a place which will forever be special to you and in your prayers or difficult times in your imagination you will remember the sublime Presence.

Already you can hear excited voices as people gather to greet Jesus.

You see the crowd approach up the road, the way is barred, you are confronted with the world again.

When they become close a silence falls and a man moves forward, and approaches Jesus.

He has his hands on the shoulders of a boy whom he gently steers towards Jesus.

You recognise them; the father had asked you to cure his son before you climbed the hill, but all your efforts had failed.

'Master,' he said, 'I implore you to look at my son; he is my only child. All at once a spirit will take hold of him, and give a sudden cry and throw the boy into convulsions with foaming at the mouth; it is slow to leave him, but when it does it leaves the boy worn out. I begged your disciples to cast it out, and they could not.'

You are shocked to hear Jesus say, 'Faithless and perverse generation how much longer must I be among you and put up with you? Bring your son here.'

His admonishment affects you deeply. You feel it is directed to everyone present, yourself included.

To your eyes there appears to be nothing wrong with the lad. Then he lets out a fearful cry that chills the hearts of everyone.

You are frozen with fear at the sound, and now the boy's face has become distorted and his body rigid; he hits the ground like a felled tree.

Jesus is the first to move; showing no fear he places his hands under the boy's head as the convulsions begin.

The boy's whole body is now convulsing rhythmically; his back is arched, arms and legs thrash violently, but his head is protected.

Froth appears from his blue lips as he begins to breathe again with hungry gasps.

You watch with the crowd as Jesus continues to hold the boy's head until the thrashing body becomes still and laboured breathing ceases.

The crowd is quiet, greatly disturbed even though they have seen the boy suffer many times before.

The boy's face is calm and colour has returned to his lips as he gently sleeps, his head resting in Jesus' hands.

You hear Jesus speak as he kneels over the cradled head. There is compassion in his voice but also admonition for the evil that has afflicted this child.

The lad recovers consciousness and sees the face of Jesus.

There is no sign of the confusion which usually follows a fit. He sits up and his father and Jesus help him to his feet.

An embrace from Jesus and then he is given to his father whose gratitude is beyond words; a warm kiss on Jesus' hand says it all.

Jesus must move on, and with a last look at the father and son, you follow.

33

Who is the Greatest? - Luke 9: 46-48

An argument started between them about which of them was the greatest. Jesus knew what thoughts were going through their minds, and he took a little child and set him by his side, and then said to them, 'Anyone who welcomes this little child in my name welcomes me; and anyone who welcomes me welcomes the one who sends me. For the least among you all, that is the one who is great.'

❖❖❖

Through his teaching and his compassion for the sick in mind and body, Jesus has touched the hearts and minds of many.

As one of his disciples you have been privileged to share in most of these encounters with the people.

Your confined world of fishing and village life has been enlarged to encompass wider horizons.

You have met the rich and the poor, the powerful and the discarded and many lives have been changed, not least your own.

After some doubts you now feel glad and proud to be part of what can now be called a successful mission.

Like other disciples you find yourself searching for something which you can claim as being your contribution to Jesus' success.

Your loyalty perhaps, your practicality in buying food, finding lodgings, even protecting Jesus from the demanding crowd.

A discussion arises and soon develops into a serious argument as each disciple puts himself forward as having contributed most to Jesus' popularity.

The now heated rivalry is becoming physical and those losing ground are becoming violent.

Jesus has been listening and now enters the centre of the squabbling disciples and restrains the worst before any harm is done.

To make matters worse some children have been watching this undignified scene.

You can see their uncomprehending eyes as they silently look out from behind their mothers' skirts.

Jesus has also seen the children and leaving the now quiet and somewhat embarrassed disciples, he takes a child by the hand and with the mother's permission the boy fearlessly allows Jesus to bring him to the disciples.

All are silent and watch as Jesus sits down with the child standing close to his side.

Your boasting and self importance is meaningless to this shy trusting child.

Before Jesus speaks, you sense that he, in his simple way, is going to lead you into a deeper understanding of what being a disciple really means.

'Anyone who welcomes this little child in my name welcomes me.'

Your reaction had not been one of welcome but more like embarrassed resentment at the intrusion.

The child and Jesus are looking at you, both with non judgemental eyes.

All your boasting and self importance now seems absurd.

The child is not boasting yet Jesus shows him great love, and neither have you ever heard Jesus boast of anything except his Father.

'Anyone who welcomes this little child in my name welcomes me; and anyone who welcomes me welcomes the one who sent me. For the least among you all, that is the one who is greatest.'

If you cannot welcome the child you cannot welcome him. Jesus, like the child, only wants your love, as he depends on his father's love.

The value you place on self esteem now seems unimportant. You possess nothing, all is a gift from God.

You may feel diminished, but also free from self, and now able to accept God's unconditional love.

Jesus has again deepened your understanding and you have been changed, and can enjoy a feeling of detachment from worldly values.

You were born to praise and serve God.

Take Lord, unto thyself,
My sense of self: and let it vanish utterly.
Take Lord my life,
Live thou thy life through me:

I live no longer, Lord,
But in me now thou livest;
Aye, between Thee and me, my God,
There is no longer room for 'I' and 'mine'.

Tukaram, Indian peasant
mystic 1608.

34

Martha and Mary – Luke 10: 38–42

In the course of their journey he came to a village, and a woman named Martha welcomed him into her house. She had a sister called Mary, who sat down at the Lord's feet and listened to him speaking. Now Martha who was distracted with all the serving said, 'Lord, do you not care that my sister is leaving me to do the serving all by myself? Please tell her to help me.' But the Lord answered: 'Martha, Martha,' he said, 'you worry and fret about many things, and yet few are needed, indeed only one. It is Mary who has chosen the better part; it is not to be taken from her.'

❖❖❖

Jesus with his disciples is entering Bethany, a small village near Jerusalem.

On the outskirts live the sisters Martha and Mary.

Martha stands alone on the roadside near her home waiting for Jesus.

She must speak with him before he reaches the villagers who are gathered in the market place to greet him.

At last he arrives and with some trepidation she approaches Jesus and invites him into her home.

He senses that this is no ordinary show of hospitality; her pleading eyes and tone of voice touch his heart and he accepts her invitation.

Because of the gravity of her demeanour, Jesus asks the disciples to remain outside while he follows Martha into her home.

Stepping from the bright sunlight, the darkness of the room at first prevents Jesus from seeing the figure of a woman who remains seated on the floor.

Martha introduces her sister Mary; the heavily veiled woman greets Jesus with a timid glance.

Jesus without ceremony sits beside her, but Martha remains standing.

Apart from the cushions on which they sit the room is empty except for a low wooden table in the centre.

Jesus waits for the sisters to speak, but their eyes are downcast and the room is silent.

Martha wants her sister to speak but cannot tolerate the silence any longer and says she must get something for Jesus to eat.

Mary remains silently seated with Jesus.

He waits, and slowly she raises her head and looks into his eyes.

There are tears spilling down her cheeks, heavy make-up begins to smudge in dark streaks down her face.

From under her plain shawl Jesus can now see the coloured hair and gaudy dress, the many bangles and bracelets that hang on her wrists.

Jesus reaches out and places his hand on her shoulder; she hears her name and looks up.

'Mary,' is all Jesus says but this releases all her inner turmoil.

He listens to her and his concern encourages her to hide nothing from him.

Her life is in serious disorder, what hope can Jesus give her?

When she has finished she looks into his eyes fearing rejection but finding total acceptance.

Already she feels changed, a deep peace renders her silent. Jesus and Mary share this peace together.

Her tears have now ceased and Mary can smile again.

Her composure enables Jesus to enlighten her on the true nature of God and how he is the fulfilment of all the prophecies.

His words inflame her heart, a new life is opening before her.

Martha appears, a tray of food in her hands which she places on the table, 'Lord, do you not care that my sister is leaving me to do the serving all by myself? Please tell her to help me.'

Martha had desperately wanted her sister to speak to Jesus but when the encounter became real she escaped into practicalities.

'Martha, Martha,' Jesus says, and with fond acceptance tells her, 'you worry and fret about so many things which are unnecessary, Mary has dealt with the important things, let her be.'

In spite of her escape into the kitchen, the deep concern she had for her sister has now been eased beyond expectation.

The sister she feared lost forever has returned.

Martha forgets the tray of food and embraces Mary with joyful tears.

Martha looks at the loving face of Jesus, takes his hand and kisses it gently with deep gratitude.

Now Jesus, a broad smile on his face, looks towards the food on the table and Martha responds with delight.

35

The Ten Lepers – Luke 17: 11–19

Now it happened that on the way to Jerusalem he was travelling in the borderlands of Samaria and Galilee. As he entered one of the villages, ten men suffering from a virulent skin disease came to meet him. They stood some way off and called to him, 'Jesus! Master! Take pity on us.' When he saw them he said, 'Go and show yourselves to the priests.' Now as they were going away they were cleansed. Finding himself cured, one of them turned back, praising God at the top of his voice and threw himself prostrate at the feet of Jesus and thanked him. The man was a Samaritan. This led Jesus to say, 'Were not all ten made clean? The other nine, where are they? It seems that not one has come back to give praise to God, except this foreigner.' And he said to the man, 'Stand up and go on your way. Your faith has saved you.'

❖❖❖

Can you imagine now, that you belong to a group of lepers living at the time of Jesus?

There are ten of you, men and women.

You have been together for many years, ever since that awful day you discovered that you had leprosy.

You are together because you refuse to live in a leper colony; as long as you obeyed the rules for lepers you could wander the countryside and stay as close to society as you possibly could.

You all miss your friends and relatives; you do see them, but only from the distance. Some of them leave food for you outside the village. They leave you old clothes to wear after you have burnt the old ones.

You can't work; anything you touch is burnt.

Every day you roam together about the countryside, total outcasts, nothing to do but sleep, eat, drink and talk of the days before you were a leper.

The awful, dreaded disease has developed over the years. Your skin is as white as snow, flaking off; lumps have grown all over your face and body; your hands and feet are bandaged up to protect them. There is no feeling in your fingers and toes and you could damage them without knowing. Some of your colleagues have lost toes and fingers, some faces are badly disfigured having lost ears, noses and lips. You are all repulsive to other people. No one cares about you except a few relatives. The rest shout at you. Children throw stones, dogs bark at you. If you see people approaching, you must ring a leper's bell and shout, 'Unclean.'

You can only talk of the old days; you don't have a future, only the slow development of leprosy, then death and burial out in the wilderness by your colleagues.

Today is different; there is a feeling in your heart you thought would never return. A glimmer of hope.

You have heard that Jesus of Nazareth is on his way to Jerusalem and is expected to pass through your village.

The village where your home used to be. You spent your childhood here and used to have a family, a job you were good at and a home you had loved.

Now what do you have? Nine companions as helpless as yourself, just waiting for death.

You can just see the house where you used to live. Your ageing parents are sitting outside; they can't see you, you don't want them to. Children are playing; they belong to you, but no longer; never will you hold them again or feel them kiss your face.

Your heart longs for them, but the thought of them being repulsed by your appearance makes you stay well away. They will grow up without you now, and your parents grow old without your support. But most of all you miss your spouse, someone to love.

There is a crowd of people behind you coming along the road to the village. One man stands out: it's Jesus; you know immediately – there is no mistaking him.

But you all keep your distance and get off the road. You start calling to him. 'Jesus, Master, take pity on us.' If only he would stop and listen – can he hear you? There are so many people around him talking and laughing.

Yes, he has stopped and is looking at you. He has heard you even though you only spoke once. It's as if he knows you and expected to see you.

'Go and show yourselves to the high priest.' His voice rings out clear as a bell.

Did you hear him right? People only go to the high priest to gain proof that they have been healed.

Jesus and the crowd are moving on into the village.

You stand looking at each other. 'We must do as he says, let's go to the priest and hear his judgement.'

As you hurry away you notice that feeling is coming back into your hands and feet.

You look at the others; colour has returned to their skin, the ugly lumps have gone.

You can feel your face, the skin is smooth. You are all cured.

There are great shouts of joy and excitement as you rush towards the priest's house.

But you have stopped, the man you have just left, Jesus, is on your mind. He was the source of all this happiness.

You turn back to find Jesus. At the top of your voice you shout, 'Blessed be God, blessed be His holy name.'

Jesus has heard you and you can see him waiting for you. You can go close to him now, and you throw yourself down at his feet and thank him with your whole heart. What he has done for you today is beyond anything you could have imagined. He has given you your life again.

You hear Jesus ask you, 'Where are the others? Were they not healed as well? Are you the only one to praise and thank God?'

You cannot speak for them, all you know is that this man has heard your cry and answered, answered in a way you could never have imagined.

Jesus is speaking to you, telling you to stand up, to go on your way; your faith has saved you.

Now you begin to realise fully what has happened: not only is your body healthy again, but now you can go home to your family, you will be accepted again in the village, you can find work and, most wonderful of all, you can embrace your spouse and children again, feel their young faces next to yours.

You are reborn and how much you value your new life is beyond words.

For the rest of your life everything will be a precious gift from God. The Lord is your shepherd, therefore you lack nothing.

36

Zacchaeus – Luke 19: 1–10

He entered Jericho and was going through the town and suddenly a man whose name was Zacchaeus made his appearance; he was one of the senior tax collectors and a wealthy man. He was anxious to see what kind of man Jesus was, but he was too short and could not see him for the crowd, so he ran ahead and climbed a sycamore tree to catch a glimpse of Jesus who was to pass that way. When Jesus reached the spot he looked up and spoke to him, 'Zacchaeus, come down. Hurry, because I am to stay at your house today.' And he hurried down and welcomed him joyfully. They all complained when they saw what was happening. 'He has gone to stay at a sinner's house,' they said. But Zacchaeus stood his ground and said to Jesus, 'Look, sir, I am going to give half my property to the poor, and if I have cheated anybody I will pay him back four times the amount.' And Jesus said to him, 'Today, salvation has come to this house, because this man too is a son of Abraham, for the Son of Man has come to seek out and save what was lost.'

❖ ❖ ❖

Jesus enters the town of Jericho. An oasis in the desert. Pure spring water nourishes beautiful palm trees which fill the town with their graceful fronds. Can you see them as they move in the breeze which comes from the desert?

Crowds of people are lining the streets; see their colourful clothes as they jostle to get near the front.

Some are in the sunshine, others in the shade of the trees.

Jesus is walking in the middle of the road, in the company of his disciples.

There is an atmosphere of great interest and curiosity.

Some shout a welcome, others are silent; this man has brought new ideas that have made them think and question. He has strange powers, he was talked about all over the country, and now here he is in their streets. What will happen now he's here? There are many reports of things he has done, and things said. There are good and bad reports: many speak of his healing powers and are full of praise and gratitude, but others have been offended by some of the things he said.

You can see there is one person who is struggling more than others to get a glimpse of Jesus. A short, rather insignificant man, he is trying to see Jesus between the people lining the street.

You notice that no one makes room for him or lets him through, even though he is much shorter than they are.

There seems hostility and open dislike for him.

He seems quite used to this rejection.

He is better dressed than most people; he wears gold around his neck, rings on his fingers and fine linen.

He is rich, very rich but he has no respect from his neighbours.

He has made his money working for the hated Romans; no one can like him for this, some even hate and despise him.

He accepts this; it's a price he's prepared to pay for collecting taxes from his own people to maintain the occupying Roman army whom they hate and fear.

He had become rich not only through receiving wages from Rome but also by deceiving the people and making them pay more than they owed, and kept it for himself. He knew many could hardly afford to pay, but he ordered all the tax gatherers under him to show no mercy. All the money came into his hands. He had become rich.

He made people, his own countrymen, pay for the upkeep of an army that occupied their country and made them second class citizens. He was lucky the Zealots hadn't cut his throat.

Why was Zacchaeus interested in Jesus?

He knew this man had touched him deeply. He felt troubled yet excited by his teaching. He knew that Jesus had said that it was easier for a camel to pass through the eye of a needle than for a rich man to enter the kingdom of heaven.

This had disturbed him, but what alternative was Jesus offering?

For some time he had become disillusioned with his life: he felt lonely, excluded, an outcast. What other life was Jesus offering?

Somehow, he knew that Jesus could give him what he was looking for.

But he can't even see Jesus, let alone speak to him. None will let him through. He knows Jesus will be passing a large sycamore tree which is easy to climb; he had done it many times when he was a boy.

He runs along the back of the crowd and comes to the tree.

He clambers up the familiar branches and is high above the heads of the people below.

Now he can see Jesus coming along the road, a dark haired man, simply dressed, a look of poverty, but dignity as well. His face kindly but serious.

Zacchaeus is feeling excited; soon this amazing man will be only a few feet beneath him.

Now Jesus' head is just below his own.

Suddenly his heart pounds, Jesus has stopped and turned his face up to look into Zacchaeus' face. Their eyes meet.

There is no sign of surprise in Jesus' face. Zacchaeus hears a friendly voice say, 'Come down from there, Zacchaeus, you are to be my host today.'

It was as if Jesus had expected to see him in the tree.

He is stunned to hear his name spoken in such friendly tones.

He is speechless but responds immediately and gets down from the tree as quickly as he can.

He feels thrilled and greatly honoured.

He shows Jesus the way to his house. This is beyond all expectation.

He opens the large carved door and invites Jesus to enter. He is not used to visitors but good hospitality comes naturally to him. He has mixed feelings. Should he be proud or ashamed of his luxurious house?

The crowd has followed and are looking in through the window; they are murmuring, why has Jesus come here of all places? Surely he can see what kind of man Zacchaeus is: no one likes him, everyone knows he is a thief and traitor. The most hated man in Jericho. Even his fellow tax collectors hold him in contempt.

In spite of their protests, Jesus has invited himself into this man's home.

Can you visualise Jesus sitting in this well-furnished room? He sits on soft, expensive cushions, his bare feet on thick, beautiful carpets. On the walls hang colourful tapestries. A fountain splashes in the courtyard behind him. He is eating and drinking out of gold cups and plates.

The people at the window have never dared to look inside the house; now they realise Zacchaeus is even wealthier than they thought. He is more like a Pagan Roman than a Jew.

Zacchaeus is delighted to play the host to this famous, intriguing man who everyone wants to meet.

He brings more wine and cakes, coffee and anything he can find and places them on the low table before Jesus.

They both sit and eat and drink together.

The people at the window become quiet – what is Zacchaeus saying to Jesus? They hear him speak. 'I am a rich man, Rabbi. I have all I want, but don't feel fulfilled. You say there is more to life than riches. What is this other kingdom you talk about? Where can I find it? I long to be in it, with you. I would gladly leave all this luxury and wealth to find it. I've already decided to give half of all of this to the poor, and those I cheated I will repay fourfold, the Roman fine for thieves.'

There are gasps of amazement from the windows.

You see Jesus place his hand on Zacchaeus' shoulder and look compassionately into his sorrowful, tearful face. This man is genuine and, in spite of his sinful past, he is worthy of forgiveness. 'Zacchaeus, you were truly lost, but I found you, and now you belong to me and are part of my family if that is what you really want.'

'Yes,' said Zacchaeus, 'There is nothing I want more.'

Jesus knows Zacchaeus has a long way to go, but he also knows what a big change has taken place in his life. He has turned his back on material wealth and has turned to him for salvation and fulfilment. He is still a human being, a son of Abraham, even though everyone hates him and thinks him to be beyond redemption, a miserable thief and traitor.

The people at the window are silent; they can only watch in disbelief. Zacchaeus looks happy; he kneels before Jesus, and he receives his blessing. There is only the sound of water tinkling in the fountain; all feel the peace that has come to the home of Zacchaeus.

37

The Resurrection of Lazarus ~

John 11: 1-44

There was a man named Lazarus who lived in the village of Bethany with the two sisters, Mary and Martha, and he was ill. It was the same Mary, the sister of the sick man Lazarus, who anointed the Lord with ointment and wiped his feet with her hair. The sisters sent this message to Jesus, 'Lord, the man you love is ill.' On receiving the message, Jesus said, 'This sickness will end not in death but in God's glory, and through it the Son of God will be glorified.'

Jesus loved Martha and her sister and Lazarus, yet when he heard that Lazarus was ill he stayed where he was for two more days before saying to the disciples, 'Let us go to Judaea.' The disciples said, 'Rabbi, it is not long since the Jews wanted to stone you; are you going back again?' Jesus replied:

'Are there not twelve hours in the day?
A man can walk in the daytime without stumbling
because he has the light of this world to see by;
but if he walks at night he stumbles,
because there is no light to guide him.'

He said that and then added, 'Our friend Lazarus is resting, I am going to wake him.' The disciples said to him, 'Lord, if he is able to rest he is sure to get better.' The phrase Jesus used referred to the death of Lazarus, but they thought that by 'rest' he meant 'sleep', so Jesus put it plainly, 'Lazarus is dead; and for your sake I am glad I was not there because now you will believe. But let us go to him.' Then Thomas, known as the Twin, said to the other disciples, 'Let us go too, and die with him.'

On arriving, Jesus found that Lazarus had been in the tomb for four days already. Bethany is only about two miles from Jerusalem, and many Jews had come to Martha and Mary to sympathise with them over their brother. When Martha heard that Jesus had come she went to meet him. Mary remained sitting in the house. Martha said to Jesus, 'If you had been here, my brother would not have died, but I know that, even now, whatever you ask of God, he will grant you.' 'Your brother,' said Jesus to her, 'will rise again.' Martha said, 'I know he will rise again at the resurrection on the last day.' Jesus said:

'I am the resurrection.
If anyone believes in me, even though he dies he will live,
and whoever lives and believes in me
will never die.
Do you believe in this?'

'Yes Lord,' she said 'I believe that you are the Christ, the Son of God, the one who was to come into this world.'

When she had said this, she went and called her sister Mary, saying in a low voice, 'The Master is here and wants to see you.' Hearing this, Mary got up quickly and went to him. Jesus had not yet come into the village; he was still at the place where Martha had met him. When the Jews who were in the house sympathising with Mary saw her get up so quickly and go out, they followed her, thinking that she was going to the tomb to weep there.

Mary went to Jesus, and as soon as she saw him threw herself at his feet, saying, 'Lord, if you had been there, my brother would not have died.' At the sight of her tears, and those of the Jews who followed her, Jesus said in great distress, with a sigh that came straight from the heart, 'Where have you put him?' They said, 'Lord come and see.' Jesus wept; and the Jews said, 'See how much he loved him!' But there were some who remarked, 'He opened the eyes of the blind man, could he not have prevented this man's death?' Still sighing, Jesus reached the tomb: it was a cave with a stone to close the opening. Jesus said, 'Take the stone away.' Martha said to him, 'Lord, by now he will smell; this is the fourth day.' Jesus replied, 'Have I not told you that if you believe you will see the glory of God?' So they took away the stone. Then Jesus lifted up his eyes and said:

> 'Father, I thank you for hearing my prayer.
> I knew indeed that you always hear me,
> but I speak
> for the sake of all these who stand round me,
> so that they may believe it was you who sent me.'

When he said this, he cried in a loud voice, 'Lazarus, here! Come out!' The dead man came out, his feet and hands bound with bands of stuff and a cloth round his face. Jesus said to them, 'Unbind him, let him go free.'

❖ ❖ ❖

The Resurrection of Lazarus - John 11: 1-44

Imagine that you are one of Jesus' disciples and are on the far side of the river Jordan. You are glad to be here, far away from Jerusalem which has become a dangerous place for Jesus and yourself. Last time you were there the people had stoned him and the Temple authorities wanted him arrested.

While in Jerusalem he had made astonishing claims. He had declared openly and clearly that he was the Son of God, that he was at one with the Father, and, even more astounding, he had the power to grant everyone eternal life.

You had been taken aback hearing Jesus say such outlandish things, but your love and respect overcame your anxiety and kept you loyal.

So now you feel safe, well away from Jerusalem. A message arrives from two women you know well, Mary and Martha; you have visited their home several times.

The news is not good; Lazarus, their brother is ill. The news alarms you, not only because Lazarus was ill, but would Jesus respond to this call and return to Bethany which was very close to Jerusalem?

You feel relieved to hear Jesus say, 'This sickness will not end in death but in God's glory, and through it the Son of God will be glorified.'

'The Son of God,' you know now that he means himself. Again he affirms his divine nature, but how, in what way will he be glorified?

You know how much Jesus loves Mary, Martha and Lazarus, but to your relief and surprise for two days there is no response from him.

Then on the third day Jesus says, 'Let us go to Judaea.'

Everyone including yourself remind him how hostile and dangerous Jerusalem has become, his life will be in danger.

His reply is simple but profound. Now is the time for him to act, as a man can move freely in daylight better than he can at night; now is his day when he must act.

Then a momentary relief when Jesus tells you that Lazarus is resting and he is going to wake him. You seize the chance to change his mind and say that restful sleep is a sure sign of recovery.

No it's not to be, Jesus changes the word 'resting' to 'dead' and nothing will stop him returning to Jerusalem. He says he is glad he waited until Lazarus died because now you will truly believe.

You don't fully understand, but you are familiar now with his extreme remarks and statements about himself.

You know from experience no one can prevent him from acting once his mind is set.

Thomas then solves your dilemma and says, 'Let us go too and die with him.' You all agree to this, a very serious and possibly fatal decision. You are prepared to risk your life to stay loyal to Jesus. You have come this far, now he is leading you into further uncharted regions.

By the time you get to Bethany, two miles from Jerusalem, you learn that Lazarus has been entombed for four days, and the mourners are still comforting the family.

This all has the makings of disaster; what is the purpose of taking such a dangerous risk in coming here? There is nothing Jesus can do now.

Martha appears before you get to the house and comes up to Jesus. You can see her tear-stained face, the tiredness shows; after the long devoted care for her sick brother, she was always the active one and got things done.

The Resurrection of Lazarus - John 11: 1-44

She is remonstrating with Jesus, 'If you had been here,' she says, 'my brother would not have died, but I know that even now, whatever you ask of God He will grant you.'

You sense that Martha has a deeper awareness of Jesus' power than you or the other disciples. What does she think he can do? She knows how closely Jesus is united with God whom he calls his father.

Jesus comforts Martha and holds her in his arms, and says to her, 'Your brother will rise again.' She looks up into his face, yes she believes he will rise again at the resurrection on the last day, but that is a long way off.

Jesus, still holding her, looks at her face close to his own and tells her, 'I am the resurrection, and anyone who has faith in me will never die, whether a person lives or dies his faith and trust will give them eternal life.'

Jesus asks her, 'Do you believe this?'

Martha looks up at Jesus, her tearful eyes full of love, and confirms her trust in him. 'Yes Lord, I believe that you are the Christ, the Son of God, the one who was to come into this world.'

You listen to these words from Martha. When you left Jerusalem these same claims made by Jesus nearly cost him his life, now you are hearing it confirmed; the seed Jesus planted has taken root in the people.

You sense anything could happen now; what it will be you cannot imagine.

Martha's sad face changes to excitement and she breaks away from Jesus and runs back to the house where she tells her sister Mary that Jesus is outside and wants to see her. She whispers this in Mary's ear, not being sure of the reaction of the other women.

Mary is sitting inert with grief in the room where she had often sat at Jesus' feet, listening to him, sharing her thoughts and feelings. He had rescued her from the prison of a sinful life.

Ever since she had sent the message, she had waited, but Jesus had not come and she had watched her brother die. She felt hurt and sad. Why hadn't he come?

When she hears Martha's words, without hesitation she leaves the room followed by the other women; she has been longing for this moment, now he is here, but it's too late.

Jesus hears again the reproach, 'If you had been here my brother would not have died.' She weeps bitterly; her face is wet with tears as Jesus raises her up and holds her in his arms.

You can see that Jesus is deeply affected by Mary's grief and with a deep sigh he asks her, 'Where have you put him?'

You are surprised when not just Mary but all the mourners encourage Jesus to 'come and see.'

Now escorted by Mary and Martha, Jesus makes his way to Lazarus' tomb, and you follow behind.

Jesus is now deeply affected and you see the tears run down his cheeks. He is grieving for a dear friend, and shares the deep sadness of the family.

He has revealed himself to be the Son of God, making himself divine, but before you is a very human man with deep human emotions caused by a great sense of loss.

Some like yourself are touched by the deep grief you see in Jesus, but even now on this occasion of deep sadness some heartlessly use scornful words, 'He opened the eyes of the blind man, could he not have prevented this man's death?'

The Resurrection of Lazarus - John 11: 1–44

Jesus hears the hurtful remarks, but with grieving sighs, he goes with the family to a nearby cave, the tomb of Lazarus, and with authority he orders the stone to be removed from the entrance.

No one expected this and Martha looks shocked and cannot help reminding Jesus that her brother has been dead four days; the body will be in a bad condition and smell.

Jesus consoles her and says, 'Have I not told you that if you believe you will see the glory of God?'

So you and the disciples remove the heavy stone. Hear the rumbling sound of stone on stone as it rolls in its gully.

Jesus moves to the tomb's entrance then turns to face the crowd of mourners, and again he affirms his divine relationship with God, 'Father, I thank you for hearing my prayer. I knew indeed that you always hear me, but I speak for the sake of all these who stand round me, so that they may believe it was you who sent me.'

You begin to feel afraid; what is going to happen?

Jesus turns towards the tomb's entrance and with a deafening shout that echoes deep within the tomb he calls out to Lazarus, 'Lazarus, here! Come out!'

Is Jesus mad? This is impossible, but as the echoes of his voice fade, out of the darkness appears a figure struggling with the bandages that bind him. It's Lazarus, with one loud gasp everyone; falls to their knees. Afraid and astounded.

The power of Jesus is far greater than you could ever have imagined.

You remain on your knees; it feels natural to worship such a man.

Jesus lifts you up and asks you to help Lazarus to get the bandages off so that he will be free.

38

The Anointing at Bethany –

John 12: 1–11

Six days before the Passover, Jesus went to Bethany, where Lazarus was, whom he had raised from the dead. They gave a dinner for him there. Martha waited on them and Lazarus was among those at table. Mary brought in a pound of very costly ointment, pure nard, and with it anointed the feet of Jesus, wiping them with her hair. The house was full of the scent of the ointment. Then Judas Iscariot – one of his disciples, the man who was to betray him – said, 'Why wasn't this ointment sold for three hundred denarii, and the money given to the poor?' He said this, not because he cared about the poor, but because he was a thief, he was in charge of the common fund and used to help himself to the contributions. So Jesus said, 'Leave her alone; she had to keep this scent for the day of my burial. You have the poor with you always, you will not always have me.'

Meanwhile a large number of Jews heard that he was there and came not only on account of Jesus but also to see Lazarus whom he had raised from the dead. Then the chief priests decided to kill Lazarus as well, since it was on his account that many of the Jews were leaving them and believing in Jesus.

❖❖❖

The Anointing at Bethany - John 12: 1-11

Ever since Jesus had revealed his divine power by raising Lazarus from the dead, his life has been in great danger. You left Jerusalem with him and spent some time on the edge of the desert in a town called Ephraim.

The Passover is drawing near when all must return to the Temple. In spite of the danger, Jesus has decided to return to Jerusalem and you and the rest of the disciples have accompanied him.

Your last visit to Jerusalem was to the home of Lazarus in Bethany, and now you are here again.

When you arrived you were filled again with great respect for Jesus; there is the tomb where Lazarus had been interred, and from where Jesus had called him back to life.

You had helped with trembling fingers to remove the bandages which then gave Lazarus his freedom.

To meet Lazarus again will confirm to you that it had not all been a dream or deception.

All three members of the family come to greet you. The two adoring sisters are first to embrace Jesus, then they make way for Lazarus who goes down on one knee in homage to Jesus, as if he was truly a king.

Jesus raises him to his feet and embraces him, his old friend.

You all enter the house – it would be unwise to be seen by too many people; news travels fast in Jerusalem.

Martha has prepared a meal. You know it will be good because you have enjoyed her cooking many times before.

The door is shut. You are all present around the table, and there is Lazarus, beaming with pleasure, a changed man. Every moment now is precious to him; he lives for the moment, just to be alive makes him grateful to God. He deeply appreciates the gift of life and the world in which he lives. He finds great peace and joy in the love of family and friends and the bond between Jesus and himself is eternal.

Picture this happy, peaceful scene. The threats and dangers are forgotten. All around the table eat and drink together. The food was as good as you expected, the talk is easy and you are all glad to be here together among friends

Sometimes a silence fills the room, and you, while seated at the table, let your eyes wander. You can see dust particles floating in a shaft of sunlight, a peaceful moment.

You take a sip of wine. You feel content: good food and wine, your closest friends are with you and Jesus is safe.

There is movement in the room, Mary is holding a jar of perfumed Nard, a very expensive balm only used on special occasions, an unction to soothe and console.

You watch her move close to Jesus as he reclines near the table.

The room remains silent as Mary goes down on her knees by Jesus' feet. No one speaks. In your heart you feel that what is about to happen will be fitting and proper.

Mary breaks the seal and takes the lid off the jar.

Jesus remains composed.

The air is filled with a lovely perfume that makes you breathe deeply, taking the fragrance deep into your lungs.

The beauty of the moment is enhanced as Mary gently anoints Jesus' feet. Her hands lovingly smear the ointment over his instep, his toes, his heels and the soles of his feet.

Your heart warms towards Mary. She is honouring your beloved Jesus. Her actions say more than words ever could.

The jar is empty, nothing saved. Mary caresses his feet until all the unction is gone, only its perfume remains in the air.

Jesus who has given you so much, knows also how to receive.

Jesus feels at home. You all come from different backgrounds but through your common love for Jesus you feel like one family, your true family. 'The swallow has found its nest.' You feel at home.

To complete her task of love, Mary must wipe any excess from Jesus' feet.

You watch Mary who is taking the pin from her hair which then falls in long dark curls onto her shoulders. She leans forward and her hair covers Jesus' feet as she gently wipes them. See her hair becoming even darker as the oil makes it shine.

'What a waste of money!' It's Judas, the treasurer. The intimacy of the moment is shattered, never to be regained. 'Why wasn't this ointment sold for three hundred denarii and the money given to the poor?'

The insult angers you; you know he isn't thinking about the poor, only his own dishonest gains.

Mary, still at Jesus' feet, looks embarrassed and looks at Jesus. He sees the tears in her eyes.

'Leave her alone, she had to keep this scent for the day of my burial. You have the poor with you always, you will not always have me.'

The atmosphere in the room has changed. Judas has deliberately spoiled a beautiful moment, and like a knife in your stomach

Judas' hostility reminds you of the danger that awaits Jesus and the threat to his life.

To confirm your fears, people you hadn't noticed until now who had come to view Lazarus are already sloping off to inform the Temple authorities.

39

The Messiah Enters Jerusalem – John 12: 12–19

The next day the crowds who had come up for the festival heard that Jesus was on his way to Jerusalem. They took branches of palm and went out to meet him, shouting, 'Hosanna! Blessings on the King of Israel, who comes in the name of the Lord.' Jesus found a young donkey and mounted it – as scripture says: Do not be afraid, daughter of Zion; see, your king is coming, mounted on the colt of a donkey. At the time his disciples did not understand this, but later, after Jesus had been glorified, they remembered that this had been written about him and that this was in fact how they had received him. All who had been with him when he called Lazarus out of the tomb and raised him from the dead were telling how they had witnessed it; it was because of this, too, that the crowd came out to meet him; they had heard that he had given this sign. Then the Pharisees said to one another, 'You see, there is nothing you can do; look, the whole world is running after him.'

❖❖❖

For six days, you and Jesus with the rest of the disciples have been staying in the house of Lazarus. It has been a quiet time, you could say a time of contemplation.

Jesus has created a family, and you are a welcome member. It has been a valuable time to understand and appreciate the divinity and humanity of Jesus.

He is at the Zenith of his fame and popularity by revealing his powerful relationship with God whom he calls father. His resurrection of Lazarus from the tomb four days after his death had dismissed any doubts concerning his Messiahship. The man who called you from your fishing nets has led you into deep unfathomable waters.

He has won the hearts and minds of thousands in Jerusalem and the surrounding districts.

You know this popularity is a mixed blessing. To the people he is their beloved saviour but to the Temple authorities he is a threat. They despise his liberating spirit, and the people are calling him king; the Romans will crush any uprising without mercy; they and the Temple are in great danger. Jesus has defeated the Pharisees' attempts to denigrate him; instead the people love and respect him.

And now, the Passover is to be celebrated and Jesus wants to go to the Temple in Jerusalem. For days you have seen people passing on their way to the Temple. The city will become crowded with devoted Jews.

You accompany Jesus as he leaves the home of Lazarus, Mary and Martha and you all set off to Jerusalem.

As you approach the Temple Gate you can see people on the walls and along the road; they are calling Jesus' name.

The Messiah Enters Jerusalem - John 12: 12-19

As you get nearer to the crowded gateway people get more excited and are shouting, 'Blessings on the King of Israel, who comes in the name of the Lord.'

Jesus has stopped beside you. He realised that what waits for him in Jerusalem could be the ultimate event in his life, but the outcome is unknown.

He sees a young donkey grazing at the roadside and asks you to bring it to him. You have often seen him ride a donkey when tired but this is only a short walk between the cheering crowds. They want him to be their King.

You don't question, but place your coat on the donkey and help Jesus mount.

They have taken down palm branches and placed them on the ground for the donkey to walk on. They also wave them and shout, a tumultuous noise of excited people, full of expectation and hope.

But you know that their joyful shouts inflame the hatred of the Sanhedrin.

You feel things are getting out of control, the people are creating a situation which could overpower Jesus and be catastrophic.

Still they shout adoringly and wave palms. This man has proved beyond doubt that he has divine powers, culminating in his resurrection of Lazarus. A miracle which has surpassed all others.

You try and keep the crowds back and make the way clear.

It is then among the crowd you see the cold watchful eyes of the Pharisees, standing at the back of the crowd. Like secret police they watch and with almost a note of defeat in their voices they ask, 'What can we do? The whole world is running after him.'

He must be stopped, but they feel powerless, they cannot change or destroy the people's adoration.

The people are calling him King; this could be their only hope. Rome will not tolerate any such claim and will kill anyone who makes such a claim against Caesar. The Romans will destroy him and they the guardians of Judaism will help them do it.

40

Jesus Washes the Disciples' Feet

~ John 13: 1-5

Before the festival of the Passover, Jesus knew that his hour had come to pass from this world to the Father. He had always loved those who were his in the world, but now he showed how perfect his love was.

They were at supper, and the devil had already put it into the mind of Judas Iscariot, son of Simon, to betray him. Jesus knew that the Father had put everything into his hands, and that he had come from God and was returning to God, and he got up from the table, removed his outer garments and, taking a towel, wrapped it round his waist. He then poured water into a basin and began to wash the disciples' feet and to wipe them with the towel he was wearing.

❖❖❖

Imagine Jesus has asked you to prepare a room in which he and his disciples can celebrate the Passover meal.

You have put a long table in the middle of a room, wooden benches on either side. The table is set for thirteen places.

On the table you place bowls of fruit, wine cups, bread, cheese and candlesticks with new candles.

On a side table you place a large bowl, a jug of water and a towel; a servant will be at hand if anyone wants to wash.

And now the room is full of men, all Jesus' disciples are present and seated at the table. Jesus is in the centre, and you are sitting near the end of the table.

You are happy to be in the company of Jesus, especially at this celebration, the escape from Egypt and slavery after hundreds of years.

Look at the table before you, the plates, wine in your cup, the candle flame. Hear the murmur of men's voices.

But there is a subdued atmosphere. Things have changed; gradually the Temple authorities have become openly hostile; you know there is a real threat to Jesus' life.

You look at Jesus. You and the disciples have grown to love and respect Jesus. Over the last three years you have been overwhelmed by many things he has said and done. His friendship has changed you, you have been uprooted, and now what does the future hold?

Something tells you that it's all over; tonight this feast will mark the end and show you the way forward.

Then, while everyone is talking and eating, you are surprised to see Jesus leave his place at the table and go towards the side table where you have placed the bowl, the jug of water and the towel.

Jesus Washes the Disciples' Feet – John 13: 1–5

Now you are really surprised. Jesus wraps the towel round his waist and picks up the bowl and jug, and walks towards the disciples.

You feel like protesting; this is the work of slaves, work which even slaves can refuse to do.

But it's too late. You can't believe your eyes; you see Jesus go to the disciple at the end of the table, kneel down and begin to wash his feet.

When finished, Jesus now moves towards you. He asks you to turn around from the table and face him.

He kneels before you. He unties the strap on your right foot, then your left.

You are looking at the top of his head; see his broad shoulders, his back as he bends over your feet.

You hear yourself protesting; you don't feel worthy of such loving respect.

But Jesus looks into your eyes and says, 'If you cannot permit me to wash your feet, I will feel rejected and we can no longer be friends.'

Immediately you know you desperately want to stay with Jesus in close companionship, and are more than willing to let him wash your feet.

You learn from Jesus' humility that indeed he came to serve, and he wants you to do the same.

Your feet are in the bowl. Feel the water as Jesus pours it over your feet. Hear the gentle splashing.

Look at Jesus' hands, carpenter's hands, some callouses where he used the saw and plane. Perhaps a scar or two where the chisel slipped.

You have seen these same hands heal the sick, cure the blind, even raise the dead.

These hands enabled you to feed hundreds of people with what you thought could only feed a few.

Hands that had often been still while he prayed to his Father.

These hands soon to be pierced by Roman nails.

These hands were now washing the dirt from off your feet.

During the three years you have spent with Jesus, you have made mistakes, been slow in comprehending; even resentment and impatience made you doubt many times.

But now this action of Jesus, you realise, is a profound expression of his love and respect for you, with all your faults.

You feel humbled by his astounding humility.

Jesus is now drying your feet with his towel and all you can say is, 'Thank you, my Lord, my King, my dear friend.'

Jesus has finished. You watch him stand, collect his jug and bowl and move to your friend Judas sitting next to you.

"His state was divine, yet he did not cling to his equality with God but emptied himself to assume the condition of a slave, and became as men are; and being as men are, he was humbler yet, even accepting death, death on a cross." Phil 2: 6–8

41

The Eucharist – Matthew 26: 26-29

Now as they were eating, Jesus took bread, and when he had said the blessing he broke it and gave it to the disciples. 'Take it and eat,' he said. 'This is my body.' Then he took a cup, and when he had given thanks he handed it to them saying, 'Drink from this, all of you, for this is my blood, the blood of the covenant, poured out for many for the forgiveness of sins. From now on, I tell you, I shall never again drink wine until the day I drink the new wine with you in the kingdom of my Father.'

❖❖❖

After Jesus has washed all the disciples' feet, he goes to the side of the room and places the jug and bowl on the table which you had placed there. He removes the towel from around his waist and puts it on the table.

There is low murmuring in the room as you watch Jesus take his seat again at the table.

The meal has come to an end. A servant begins to clear the table. Watch him collect all the wine cups, the plates, the bread, cheese and fruit.

When he comes to Jesus you hear Jesus request that the servant leaves his wine cup and his bread.

All have become quiet; the servant has finished; the clatter of dishes has stopped.

The room is in silence.

You watch as Jesus takes the bread left before him. He offers thanks to God.

'Blessed are you, Father. Through your goodness we have this bread to eat which the earth has given to us and human hands have made.'

You watch him break the bread into pieces and he looks at all the disciples and tells you all to eat it because tonight this has become his body.

The plate comes to you and you take a piece. See the brown crust and the soft white bread.

The bread in your mouth has been blessed by the hands of Jesus. Can you taste the crusty bread?

After the empty plate returns to Jesus you see him take the wine jug and fill his cup to the brim.

You hear him give thanks, 'Blessed are you, Father, Father of all creation. It is through your goodness that we have this wine to drink, fruit of the vine and work of men's hands.'

He looks up and down the table at all the disciples again and he tells you to drink from his cup because tonight this has become his blood which is to be shed for the forgiveness of sins and the declaration of his new kingdom.

The cup is passed around the table; when it comes to you, you look into the cup. See the ruby red wine, smell its fragrance.

You look up and Jesus encourages you to drink. Taste the sweet bouquet.

Time stands still, an eternal moment; you feel at one with Jesus.

You pass on the cup to the person next to you and the empty cup returns to Jesus.

There is peaceful silence and all are looking at Jesus. His next words disturb you; he will never drink wine with you again, not until the new kingdom is established.

The meal is now over. Jesus stands up and you all join him singing psalms of praise. Can you hear the men's voices as their singing fills the room?

You don't understand all that has happened tonight, you just follow Jesus as he leaves the room.

The room is now silent and empty. On the table there is only an empty cup and a plate with a few crumbs of bread.

42

Gethsemane – Matthew 26: 36-46

Then Jesus came with them to a plot of land called Gethsemane, and he said to his disciples, 'Stay here while I go over there to pray.' He took Peter and the two sons of Zebedee with him. And he began to feel sadness and anguish.

Then he said to them, 'My soul is sorrowful to the point of death. Wait here and stay awake with me.' And, going on a little further, he fell on his face and prayed. 'My Father,' he said, 'if it is possible, let this cup pass me by. Nevertheless, let it be as You, not I, would have it.' He came back to the disciples and found them sleeping, and he said to Peter, 'So you had not the strength to stay awake with me for one hour? Stay awake, and pray not to be put to the test. The spirit is willing enough, but human nature is weak.' Again, a second time, he went away and prayed. 'My Father,' he said, 'if this cup cannot pass by, but I must drink it, Your will be done!' And he came back again and found them sleeping, their eyes were so heavy. Leaving them there, he went away again and prayed for the third time, repeating the same words. Then he came back to the disciples and said to them, 'You can sleep on now and have your rest. Look, the hour has come when the Son of Man is to be betrayed into the hands of sinners. Get up! Let us go! Look, my betrayer is not far away.'

❖ ❖ ❖

Gethsemane – Matthew 26: 36–46

Imagine that you have just celebrated the Passover meal with all the disciples. Jesus had made it a momentous occasion. He had made everyone feel everything was coming to an end; after tonight nothing would be the same.

He was saying goodbye, but you refuse to accept it.

You have been fully aware of a change in Jesus since you arrived in Jerusalem.

Neither you nor the rest of the disciples wanted him to come here; you knew it would be dangerous.

You had often heard him say he would meet his death in Jerusalem, so why are you here? He is the Master and you trust him.

Judas had, for some reason, left the party early, the last psalms have been sung, and now you are all leaving the upper room with Jesus, who has asked you to accompany him to his favourite place where you can pray. You know it well, a peaceful garden called Gethsemane, the other side of the Kidron valley.

You take the familiar path through the city gate near the Temple and down the valley.

You cross the stream over the small bridge. See the moon reflected in the water, hear it chattering over the stones. See the green weeds moving in the stream, the rushes near the riverbank.

You are soon on the other side of the valley and climb up into the well-known garden. The familiar olive trees cover the hillside.

Jesus leads the way up among the trees. See the gnarled grey trunks, the small leaves – are there any olives on the branches?

He stops and tells you to wait and stay awake while he goes further on where he can pray. This has been the routine many times before. Peter and the sons of Zebedee go with him.

You are glad to sit down. The ground is dry; you feel the dead leaves beneath you.

The food and wine has made you drowsy.

In the cold night air, you wrap your cloak around you and cover your head.

You look towards Jesus – there is something very wrong! Usually he is quiet when he prays, a profound stillness has always emanated from him, but not tonight.

You begin to feel very uneasy, Jesus is restless; he kneels, then he prostrates himself on the ground, his hands clutching the dry leaves.

You can hear faint groaning sounds deep in his chest.

When you look again he is standing, holding onto a branch for support. He seems to be wrestling with his thoughts. He looks tormented.

This is far from his usual peaceful prayers.

Then you hear what he is saying.

'Father, I am longing for you to let this cup of suffering and death pass me by.'

Then you also hear him say, 'But Father, I want to choose Your way. My spirit is willing but my flesh is weak; I know Your way is the right way.'

You close your eyes to escape from this disturbing scene; you just want to escape into sleep.

Gethsemane – Matthew 26: 36–46

You hear Jesus close to you. You open your eyes. He asks why you can't stay awake, stay awake and pray that you are not tempted, tempted to take the easy option.

You know what he means; you pleaded with him to avoid danger and now what you dreaded most is beginning to happen.

Jesus leaves you and returns to his place of prayer.

You can see in his face, he *is* tormented, full of sorrow; he is grieving deeply.

There is fear and dread in his eyes. Sweat is pouring off his face and down his neck like blood from a wound. It frightens you to see his agony.

Again you hear his voice, pleading with his Father to spare him from agony and death.

You see Jesus stand up and walk towards you. He wants to know if you are praying with him.

But you cannot share his struggle, his agony. You shut your eyes and pretend to be asleep.

You hear his feet in the leaves as he walks away. He is going to pray for the third time.

You open your eyes to look at him.

He is still restless and distraught. Is he wrestling with God, himself or the devil? And so it goes on, will this night ever end? Then you see a change come over him.

His face becomes the face you know; his stillness and serenity has suddenly returned at last, he is at peace with himself and his Father.

His voice is deep and calm; you hear him speak.

'Father, I have chosen the way I must take, Your will, not mine, must be done. I will tread the human road of suffering and death; it's the only way. Thy will be done.'

Your heart sinks like a stone. The night suddenly feels colder. This is what you dreaded: Jesus is not going to escape from Jerusalem. He is going to let his enemies win. What is going to happen to you now?

Jesus is returning to you again. He looks calm, composed, you could say; he even looks happy. Gone is all the torment; there is a look of victory in his eyes.

You find comfort in his face; he looks confident. His air of authority has returned, he is in control again – maybe things won't be so bad?

But your fears are awakened again. Jesus says, 'It's alright now, all temptation is passed and overcome. You can sleep; you will be safe. I will be taken away by my enemies but be brave.'

In the dark trees below you can see lanterns and torches, hear the rattle of armour and weapons, heavy feet rustling through the leaves.

Jesus is standing above you. He takes your hand and helps you to your feet and says in a confident voice, 'Come, get up and let us go and meet my betrayer and his army. This is the way it has to be; everything you have shared with me has been leading up to this moment. My Father will be with us; come, let us go.'

"Here is my servant whom I uphold, my chosen one in whom my soul delights. I have endowed him with my spirit that he may bring true justice to the nations." Isaiah 42: 1–2

43

The Arrest – Matthew 26: 47-56

He was still speaking when Judas, one of the Twelve, appeared, and with him a large number of men armed with swords and clubs, sent by the chief priests and elders of the people. Now the traitor had arranged a sign with them. 'The one I kiss,' he had said 'he is the man. Take him in charge.' So he went straight up to Jesus and said, 'Greetings, Rabbi,' and kissed him. Jesus said to him, 'My friend, do what you are here for.' Then they came forward, seized Jesus and took him in charge. At that, one of the followers of Jesus grasped his sword and drew it; he struck out at the high priest's servant, and cut off his ear. Jesus then said, 'Put your sword back, for all who draw the sword will die by the sword. Or do you think that I cannot appeal to my Father who would promptly send more than twelve legions of angels to my defence? But then, how would the scriptures be fulfilled that say this is the way it must be?' It was at this time that Jesus said to the crowds, 'Am I a brigand, that you had to set out to capture me with swords and clubs? I sat teaching in the Temple day after day and you never laid hands on me.' Now all this happened to fulfil the prophecies in scripture. Then all the disciples deserted him and ran away.

❖❖❖

Your mind is in turmoil and fear grips your heart. In the Gethsemane garden of olive trees you have witnessed Jesus as you have never seen him before. You watched him wrestle with himself; through inner turmoil he overcame his human need to avoid suffering and death.

His triumph over human weakness had been achieved through his obedience and his love for his Father.

But now there are noises in the trees below, the rustle of many feet in the leaves, people are approaching, strangely silent, only the rattle of weapons and armour. You see the lanterns and torches coming up between the trees.

A figure steps out into the clearing; you heave a sigh of relief; it's Judas. Where has he been all night, and why has he brought all these armed men to where he knows Jesus comes to pray?

Judas stands with the Temple Guard; his face is expressionless, he is searching for someone; his cold eyes find who he is looking for; you watch him walk towards Jesus, who stands next to you.

The men, armed with swords and clubs, are close behind him. You don't recognise any of them and they clearly have never seen Jesus before tonight.

They follow Judas who comes close. He greets Jesus and calls him Rabbi. You watch him embrace your beloved companion and kiss his face; he is showing love and respect.

But his actions are so incongruous; he is surrounded by armed, hostile men.

Jesus responds to this show of affection and loyalty and says, 'My friend, do what you are here for.'

He seems to be condoning what Judas is doing and can still call him friend.

The Arrest – Matthew 26: 47–56

The guards roughly push Judas aside out of the way as they force Jesus' arms behind his back and tie his wrists together with rope.

You just cannot let this happen; to see Jesus tied up like a criminal awakens your anger at this outrage against the person of Jesus.

Peter, always the first to act, has taken a sword from the sheath of a guard and strikes wildly with the ringing steel. Never having used a sword, he only manages to cut the ear off one of the high priest's servants.

Now you are all in danger, but before there is any retaliation from the Guards, Jesus in his loud, clear voice commands Peter to return the sword. This pacifies the guard; to your great relief the danger is passed.

Have we learnt nothing? 'Those who draw the sword will die by the sword,' says Jesus.

Once again Peter's way is not acceptable.

Everyone calms down; his voice has always had this effect. His powerful presence is felt stronger than ever, as he speaks to the men who have come to arrest him and take him away.

'Do you not think that I cannot appeal to my father who would promptly send more than twelve legions of angels to my defence?' The same angels you know joyfully announced his birth. 'But then how would the scriptures be fulfilled that say this is the way it must be.'

Most, if not all of the men sent to arrest him, had never heard him speak before and this is the first time they have felt his presence and air of authority.

They become silent and listen to him as he speaks in reasonable tones and gently admonishes them.

'Am I a brigand, that you had to set out to capture me with swords and clubs? I sat teaching in the Temple day after day and you never laid hands on me.'

But the guards remember their orders and their salaries promised by the Temple Authorities if they find Jesus and bring him bound and powerless to be under their authority at last.

Without ceremony they impatiently take hold of Jesus and escort him away.

The remaining guards are now looking at you; their eyes are suspicious; they reach for their swords. There is only one thing you can do; run, run as fast as you can into the trees, the olive grove which you know has thousands of trees in which you can hide and be safe. Your only escape from this awful night.

44

Jesus Before Annas –

John 18: 12–24

The cohort and its captain and the Jewish guards seized Jesus and bound him. They took him first to Annas, because Annas was the father-in-law of Caiaphas, who was high priest that year. It was Caiaphas who had suggested to the Jews, 'It is better for one man to die for the people.'

Simon Peter, with another disciple, followed Jesus. This disciple, who was known to the high priest, went with Jesus into the high priest's palace, but Peter stayed outside the door. So the other disciple, the one known to the high priest, went out, spoke to the woman who was keeping the door and brought Peter in. The maid on duty at the door said to Peter, 'Aren't you another of that man's disciples?' He answered, 'I am not.' Now it was cold, and the servants and guards had lit a charcoal fire and were standing there warming themselves; so Peter stood there too, warming himself with the others.

The high priest questioned Jesus about his disciples and his teaching. Jesus answered, 'I have spoken openly for all the world to hear; I have always taught in the synagogue and in the Temple where all the Jews meet together: I have said nothing in secret. But why ask me? Ask my hearers what I taught: they know what

I said.' At these words, one of the guards standing by gave Jesus a slap in the face, saying, 'Is that the way to answer the high priest?' Jesus replied, 'If there is something wrong in what I said, point it out; but if there is no offence in it, why do you strike me?' Then Annas sent him, still bound, to Caiaphas the high priest.

❖❖❖

After Jesus' arrest in the garden of Gethsemane, imagine that you are a disciple hiding with Peter among the olive trees, thankful for a moonless night.

You have watched all the armed men disperse and empty the clearing below.

On the other side of the Kidron valley you can see the head of the cortege nearing the Temple gate in the walls of Jerusalem. You can see Jesus, still bound, being pushed along the road. He is alone, in the power of his enemies.

You look at Peter beside you. See the anguish in his eyes which are now becoming angry.

He cannot hide any longer and with him you descend into the Kidron valley and follow your beloved master.

You both enter the city in time to see the last of the crowd enter the palace yard of Annas, the father-in-law of Caiaphas, the high priest.

You are not a stranger to Annas and his guards know you. You pass through the gates into the courtyard, leaving Peter hiding in the shadows.

The woman keeping the gate knows you and you ask her to let your friend into the courtyard where he quickly blends in with the men around a fire.

You can now enter the home of Annas, desperate to see what is happening to Jesus. You might be able to help him.

You enter the public courtroom and there stands Jesus, his head up looking at Annas on his seat of authority. His hands still bound behind his back, he stands accused, alone.

Annas looks pleased with the night's work and he enjoys questioning Jesus about his disciples and his teaching.

He is not searching for the truth but the chance to condemn.

Jesus is not cowed by Annas' authority or his hostility but looks him in the eye and says, 'I have spoken openly for all the world to hear; I have always taught in the synagogue and in the temple where all the Jews meet together; I have said nothing in secret. But why ask me? Ask my hearers what I taught; they know what I said.'

Annas looks shocked, unaccustomed to such fearless defiance; this man dares to challenge his intelligence.

A guard is aware of the threat to Annas' authority and potential humiliation and steps forward to strike Jesus in the face. 'Is that the way to answer the high priest?'

The sound of the hard slap on Jesus' cheek echoes in your mind and gives you pain.

But you feel proud when Jesus lifts his head and looks at the guard, 'If there is something wrong in what I said, point it out; but if there is no offence in it, why do you strike me?'

It's now the guard's turn to look confused, unsure what to do next.

This has become too much. Wanting to give the guard support and please Annas the others join in and begin striking Jesus on his unprotected face.

Annas in his seat looks amused, a cruel smile on his face, and says nothing.

This encourages the guards who now feel free to do what they like, even have some fun with their captive.

You are watching as one guard removes his neckerchief and covers Jesus' eyes.

Jesus stands before you, hands tied behind his back. Hard fists strike his face. Your eyes are closed but you can still hear the blows on his face.

They want him to play the prophet. 'Who struck you?' they ask.

Blood streams from Jesus' nose and drops of dark red blood fall on his garment.

You can bear no more. You cannot rescue him, what else can you do but leave this dreadful scene and see no more.

Over the noisy, cruel games, you hear Annas at last command that Jesus be taken away, to Caiaphas, the high priest.

You don't wait to see Jesus taken away. You must find Peter, but when you get outside he's nowhere to be seen, so well has he blended into the crowded courtyard.

45

Peter's Denial – Luke 22: 54–62

They seized him then and led him away, and they took him to the high priest's house. Peter followed at a distance. They had lit a fire in the middle of the courtyard and Peter sat down among them, and as he was sitting there by the blaze a servant girl saw him, peered at him, and said, 'This man was with him, too.' But he denied it. 'Woman, I do not know him,' he said. Shortly afterwards someone else saw him and said, 'You are one of them, too.' But Peter replied, 'I am not, my friend.' About an hour later another man insisted, saying, 'This fellow was certainly with him. Why, he is Galilean.' Peter said, 'My friend, I do not know what you are talking about.' At that instant, while he was still speaking, the cock crowed, and Jesus turned and looked straight at Peter, and Peter remembered Jesus' words when he said to him, 'Before the cock crows today, you will have disowned me three times.' And he went outside and wept bitterly.

❖ ❖ ❖

Jesus has been arrested in the garden of Gethsemane and taken under guard by the Roman soldiers and Temple guard.

The disciples have all fled into the night and hidden themselves for safety.

Peter has the courage to follow, at a safe distance, and is now sitting by the fire in the courtyard of the high priest.

The courtyard is full of people. Roman soldiers on night duty, servants and the Temple guard, which had arrested Jesus.

See Peter as he sits warming himself by the burning charcoal. See how it glows, the blue smoke rising into the night sky; smell the smoke in the air.

He looks furtive, his hood over his head; he doesn't want to be noticed.

The night is cold. Peter moves closer to the fire; he is trembling with fear and the cold.

A servant girl is moving among the men, giving them something hot to drink.

She comes to Peter. He looks up and at once the girl recognises him.

Peter quickly looks down, but she says out loud, 'This person was with the arrested man, he was one of his disciples.'

Peter is terrified. 'Woman, hold your tongue. I don't know him; I've nothing to do with him.'

Peter gets up quickly and moves away to another fire in the courtyard.

He tries to blend in with the soldiers and other men; he knows what danger he is in. But his courage had never let him down; he was known to be a bold man by everyone.

See Peter seated by the crackling fire; the stars above him are bright in the cold, black sky.

He dares to take a quick look at the man next to him. He has a welcome sense of relief; he knows this man, he's an old friend.

The man looks back at Peter, his face shows he recognises Peter and before Peter can stop him he blurts out, 'Peter, you were a disciple of the arrested man. I remember seeing you with him many times.'

'My friend, please keep your voice down, you are mistaken.'

Peter doesn't wait for his friend to remonstrate any further, he moves across the courtyard, nearer to the gate; there he stands in the shadows.

There is a commotion coming from the high priest's house.

Peter can see Jesus, under guard, coming towards him; he is shocked to see blood and bruising on his face.

Peter is near the gate as Jesus passes by; their eyes meet.

Jesus immediately recognises Peter, his tired eyes light up, and Peter's heart swells with love. Peter had expected to see a look of contempt or accusation, but instead Jesus looks pleased to see him.

A soldier standing by the gate notices this look of recognition exchanged by the two men.

The soldier shouts out, 'This man was with the prisoner, I can tell; he's a Galilean.'

Peter looks away from Jesus and laughing he tells the soldier, 'I don't know what you are talking about.'

His forced laughter is suddenly drowned by the loud crowing of a cockerel on the courtyard wall.

Peter turns to look at Jesus but he is gone, taken away, away into the night.

Peter leaves the courtyard; there is nothing here for him now. Overwhelmed with grief, he sits with his back against the wall.

His eyes fill with tears; he has failed; his pride is shattered. He weeps for himself and is ashamed; he has been a coward.

How can he carry on after this? When Jesus really needed him he had let him down, let him down badly.

But what makes the tears flow is the memory of the look in Jesus' eyes; there had been love and friendship and the familiar warmth of expression.

There hadn't only been warmth in Jesus' eyes, there had also been consolation.

Of course, Peter remembered the crowing cock; Jesus had foreseen all of it.

Jesus knew him better than he knew himself.

And knowing all his faults, he had loved him still.

These thoughts made his heart swell with love for his beloved master even more. The pain was intense, the tears flowed.

See Peter now crouched by the wall, hidden by the night, broken-hearted but consoled by his certainty that Jesus, wherever he was, still thought of him as a loved, but now a forgiven friend.

He could never be proud of himself again but his love and pride for Jesus was unlimited.

46

Jesus Before the Sanhedrin – Mark 14: 55–65

The chief priests and the whole Sanhedrin were looking for evidence against Jesus on which they might pass the death-sentence. But they could not find any. Several, indeed, brought false evidence against him, but their evidence was conflicting. Some stood up and submitted this false evidence against him, 'We heard him say, "I am going to destroy this Temple made by human hands, and in three days build another, not made by human hands."' But even on this point their evidence was conflicting. The high priest then stood up before the whole assembly and put this question to Jesus, 'Have you no answer to that? What is this evidence these men are bringing against you?' But he was silent and made no answer at all. The high priest put a second question to him, 'Are you the Christ,' he said, 'the Son of the Blessed One?' 'I am,' said Jesus 'and you will see the Son of Man seated at the right hand of the Power and coming with the clouds of heaven.' The high priest tore his robes. 'What need of witnesses have we now?' he said. 'You heard the blasphemy. What is your finding?' And they all gave their verdict: he deserved to die.

Some of them started spitting at him and, blindfolding him, began hitting him with their fists and shouting, 'Play the prophet!' And the attendants rained blows on him.

❖❖❖

Imagine you are that disciple who accompanied Peter to the Palace of Annas. You were unable to find Peter in the courtyard, so alone you have followed Jesus to the Palace of Caiaphas, the high priest of the Sanhedrin.

The first light of dawn is touching the horizon, the night will soon be over, but your nightmare continues.

You are now seated in the large courtroom of the Sanhedrin.

Caiaphas is now on the seat of authority. The most powerful man in the Temple hierarchy, supported by all the elders and scribes.

You can see Jesus, still bound, the front of his garment streaked with blood. His face is bruised and swollen.

Tears fill your eyes to see him so cruelly treated.

The whole Sanhedrin is eager to find evidence that will condemn Jesus; they want to destroy him now, at last, they have him in their power.

You are powerless to save him, you can voice no support in his defence but only watch and share his humiliation. There is no one to defend him; he stands alone.

This body of clever men are finding it difficult to produce any conclusive evidence against Jesus.

In desperation they flagrantly ignore the law and bring in false witnesses.

Jesus Before the Sanhedrin – Mark 14: 55–65

Some recall a statement Jesus made while speaking in the Temple.

'We heard him say', "I am going to destroy this Temple made by human hands, and in three days build another, not made by hands."'

You can remember Jesus saying these words and even a child would have known he was not talking about bricks and mortar. The evidence against Jesus is pathetic.

See Caiaphas get to his feet; he knows the trial is getting nowhere,;he takes a few paces forward, and using all the authority he can muster he demands Jesus answer these accusations.

He makes no answer, he looks at Caiaphas but remains silent.

Caiaphas looks beaten; his voice is lower and in almost imploring tones he asks, 'Are you the Christ, the son of the Holy One?'

Jesus looks into this man's sad eyes and instantly replies, 'I am, and you will see the son of man seated at the right hand of the Power and coming with the clouds of heaven.'

The room falls silent; Caiaphas looks deeply into Jesus' eyes. He wants to believe him but his pride won't let him.

In his frustration his hands grip his garment and tear open the front, like a mourner at a funeral.

This act signals the end of the matter; there will be no further discussion.

He condemns Jesus. 'What need of witnesses have we now, you heard the blasphemy? What is your finding?'

The whole Sanhedrin know what Caiaphas wants to hear and all shout, 'He deserves to die.'

There is uproar. Caiaphas returns to his seat and leaves the rabble of witnesses free to express their contempt by spitting on Jesus and repeating the game of blindfolding him, then striking his face, asking him to play the prophet.

Again you witness the cruelty and humiliation Jesus is suffering at the hands of his enemies.

This is a Temple Court; never have witnesses and members of the public been allowed to abuse a prisoner in this barbaric manner.

You despair of any justice now; Jesus is being thrown to the wolves.

They want him dead but don't have the power to execute him; they will take him before Pilate and use all their powers to manipulate him to carry out their demands.

47

Jesus Before Pilate – Luke 23: 2-7

They began their accusation by saying, 'We found this man inciting our people to revolt, opposing payment of the tribute to Caesar, and claiming to be Christ, a king.' Pilate put to him this question, 'Are you the king of the Jews?' 'It is you who say it,' he replied. Pilate then said to the chief priests and the crowd, 'I find no case against this man.' But they persisted. 'He is inflaming the people with his teaching all over Judea; it has come all the way from Galilee, where he started, down to here.' When Pilate heard this, he asked if the man were a Galilean; and finding that he came under Herod's jurisdiction he passed him over to Herod who was also in Jerusalem at that time.

❖❖❖

It's a short walk from Caiaphas' palace to the Antonine Fortress which the Romans have built close to the north wall of the temple.

You know the way and before the Temple guard removes Jesus from the palace of Caiaphas you make your way to the Fort and wait for the arrival of Jesus under guard.

You don't have to wait long; the Sanhedrin want this business over and done with as soon as possible, rushed through and completed.

You slip inside before Jesus arrives. This building contrasts with the palace of Caiaphas – it's less ornate and you instantly feel the formal efficiency of Rome.

Jesus is brought in by his armed guards, his face swollen and bruised, fresh blood staining his clothing.

Guards stand to attention and Pilate, the Roman Governor, appears.

His loose informal toga shows his unreadiness for this early morning hearing.

He has been forced to deal with this case by the Sanhedrin and resents their persistence so early in the day.

As soon as he appears they begin to shout their accusations and tell Pilate, 'We found this man inciting our people to revolt, opposing payment of the tribute to Caesar, and claiming to be Christ, a king.'

This is their ace card, making him to be a threat to Rome. You know it's a lie; he didn't oppose the imperial tax.

They fail to mention his teaching which has challenged the scribes and Pharisees, and undermined their power over the people.

Pilate looks at Jesus for the first time. He sees a man bound and beaten, alone and powerless. He bluntly asks, 'Are you the king of the Jews?' He looks mildly amused. This man before him is hardly a threat to Caesar and the Empire. How absurd to make him rise so early for this ridiculous hearing.

'I find no case against this man.' The authority in his voice is meant to be the last word and he rises to leave. You can't believe your ears; Pilate is throwing the case out of court.

But they persist, 'He is inflaming the people with his teaching all over Judea; it has come all the way from Galilee, where it started, down to here.'

They are now getting closer to the truth. It is the influence of his teaching on people's beliefs that they want to stop.

Pilate sits down and is thinking. You sense that Jesus is not going to be released that easily.

Pilate looks up. 'Is this man from Galilee?' When it's confirmed Pilate realises his chance to unburden himself from this tedious nonsense.

The accused, if from Galilee, comes under the jurisdiction of Herod, being King of Judea.

It's unfortunate for Jesus, because you know that Herod is in Jerusalem at this time.

Pilate takes the easy way out and orders the guard to take Jesus to the palace of Herod and present him to King Herod for judgement.

You are greatly disappointed with Pilate's decision. Jesus had come close to freedom only for it to be snatched away.

You feel desolate and alone as you watch the guards take Jesus from the court.

48

Jesus Before Herod – Luke 23: 8–12

Herod was delighted to see Jesus; he had heard about him and had been wanting for a long time to set eyes on him; moreover, he was hoping to see some miracle worked by him. So he questioned him at some length but without getting any reply. Meanwhile the chief priests and the scribes were there, violently pressing their accusations. Then Herod, together with his guards, treated him with contempt and made fun of him; he put a rich cloak on him and sent him back to Pilate. And though Herod and Pilate had been enemies before, they were reconciled that same day.

❖❖❖

You have followed the armed guards who have taken Jesus, under Pilate's orders, to the palace of Herod near the Joppa Gate.

You are still feeling disappointed and angry. Pilate could find no case against Jesus and had wanted to release him, but he had changed his mind under the pressure from the Sanhedrin. To evade the need to make a decision, he has transferred the case to Herod because Jesus comes under his jurisdiction.

And now you sit in Herod's court. He has always shown an interest in Jesus but didn't share his brother's hatred for him.

Jesus Before Herod – Luke 23: 8–12

Could this man standing before him be the threat his brother Herod had feared long ago and had caused him to commit the outrage of killing hundreds of infants?

This Herod holds no fear of Jesus and he is delighted to see him at last.

Over the years he has been amused and intrigued to hear stories about Jesus; to him he sounds like a great magician.

Herod feels honoured by Pilate for sending this court case to his palace. This could be very amusing and also gratifying to his self-importance.

You watch Herod leave his chair of office and approach Jesus.

Your heart aches to see the vulnerability of Jesus as he stands alone, bound and defenceless, bruised, with drops of blood still falling on his chest.

Tears spill from your eyes and you hide the sob welling up in your chest.

Herod is animated and enjoys questioning Jesus. He wants first-hand accounts of all the stories he has been hearing about him.

There remains an amused smile on his face even though Jesus is not responding to his questions, and remains silent.

So now, for his amusement Herod wants to see a miracle performed. Again, there is no response.

He is in high spirits and wonders why his brother had feared him, this pathetic, mute pretender.

But the chief priests and scribes pursue their quarry and vehemently try to convince Herod that Jesus is a threat. 'He is inflaming the people with his teaching all over Judea.'

Herod has his own opinions and only sees a fool before him and only feels contempt for the man and shows it.

He is not going to do Pilate's dirty work either. This case isn't worthy of his judgement.

To compensate for his disappointment in Jesus, and because they have told him that Jesus claims to be a king, it would be eloquent and humorous to send him back to Pilate dressed as a king. The sight of him will tell Pilate how ridiculous he considers the whole affair.

You see Herod remove his cloak and tell a guard to place it on Jesus. It hangs well on his broad shoulders and the quality of kingship is apparent even in his humiliation.

Jesus is escorted from Herod's palace and you follow the cortege back to the Antonine Fortress where Jesus will come under Pilate's authority once again.

His life is in the hands of others, there is no one to defend him and he doesn't defend himself. You understand from your personal knowledge of him that this defencelessness is because of his complete trust in his Father's love. He will be obedient and faithful to the end.

49

Jesus Before Pilate –

John 18: 28–40

They then led Jesus from the house of Caiaphas to the Praetorium. It was now morning. They did not go into the Praetorium themselves or they would be defiled and unable to eat the Passover. So Pilate came outside to them and said, 'What charge do you bring against this man?' They replied, 'If he were not a criminal, we should not be handing him over to you'. Pilate said, 'Take him yourselves, and try him by your own Law.' The Jews answered, 'We are not allowed to put a man to death.' This was to fulfil the words Jesus had spoken indicating the way he was going to die.

So Pilate went back into the Praetorium and called Jesus to him, 'Are you the king of the Jews?' he asked. Jesus replied, 'Do you ask this of your own accord, or have others spoken to you about me?' Pilate answered, 'Am I a Jew? It is your own people and the chief priests who have handed you over to me: what have you done?' Jesus replied, 'Mine is not a kingdom of this world; if my kingdom were of this world, my men would have fought to prevent my being surrendered to the Jews. But my kingdom is not of this kind.' 'So you are a king then?' said Pilate. 'It is you who say it,' answered Jesus. 'Yes, I am a king. I was born for this, I came into the world for this: to bear witness to the truth; and all who are on the side of truth listen to my voice.' 'Truth?' said

Pilate, 'What is that?'; and with that he went out again to the Jews and said, 'I find no case against him. But according to a custom of yours I should release one prisoner at the Passover; would you like me, then, to release the king of the Jews?' At this they shouted: 'Not this man,' they said 'but Barabbas'. Barabbas was a brigand.

❖❖❖

Jesus has now been brought before Pilate for the second time. You have followed him all night after his arrest in the garden of Gethsemane.

You have seen Jesus questioned and humiliated in the Roman Court and in the meaningless encounter with Herod. Now Jesus is still under arrest and being held in the Antonine Fortress where he was first questioned by Pilate.

A decision now has to be made; Pilate sending Jesus to Herod had been futile, the problem was back in Pilate's court.

The Praetorium was to be the arena where the life or death of Jesus was to be decided, the highest court of Rome in Israel.

The events of the night have exhausted you physically and mentally.

Because as a Jew you cannot enter the pagan building which would make you defiled for the Passover, you are waiting outside.

This allows your exhausted mind to drift over the events of the last twelve hours.

Another day has dawned but your mind is full of the traumatic events of the night just passed.

Jesus Before Pilate – John 18: 28–40

It is a different world you now dream of; fresh in your mind is the supper you and the disciples shared with Jesus in the upper room. You can remember the warmth and companionship, but also you recall the ominous feeling then that things were about to change.

How much they were going to change you could never have imagined.

You have seen the man whom you love and respect taken like a dangerous criminal in the night. You have seen him humiliated and physically abused by Temple guards, the high priests, even ordinary people.

Herod the custodian of Jewish law in Galilee had humiliated him and contemptuously sent him back to Pilate for him to decide his fate. This new day brings you little hope of justice.

Your despairing thoughts are broken as Pilate comes from the Praetorium to speak to the people.

You know that the crowd around you are not here to see justice but, under the influence of the Temple, they are like wolves wanting their prey.

Pilate addresses the crowd, 'What charge do you bring against this man?'

He has asked this question before and must know that there is no sound evidence to justify their absurd charges.

The crowd's answer is churlish. 'If he were not a criminal we should not be handing him over to you.'

Pilate feels the insult; this lack of respect unnerves him, and angrily he retorts, 'Take him yourselves, and try him by your own Law.'

Pilate knew this had already been attempted but Herod had sent Jesus back without sentence.

The crowd inform Pilate, 'We are not allowed to put a man to death.' They had only one desire, the death of Jesus; evidence to justify this was irrelevant and unnecessary.

Pilate could not fail to feel their cold, merciless determination to have Jesus executed.

Pilate needs time to think; his duty as Governor and deliverer of justice was being undermined by this blood-thirsty mob.

He turns his back on them and re-enters the Praetorium.

It was later that day when you spoke to a Roman guard that you learned what happened next.

Pilate asked Jesus, 'Are you the king of the Jews?' What did he want to hear? If Jesus said he was, then he could condemn him for insurrection, but he can see for himself that this man is no threat to Rome.

Jesus' response is a personal enquiry of Pilate's reason for asking such a question.

'Do you ask this of your own accord, or have others spoken to you about me?' Does Pilate ask because he really wants to know for personal satisfaction or just to justify the crowd's accusation?

Pilate is entering unknown regions; this man is speaking of another world; he is not claiming to be king of the world he knows as a Roman Governor.

Pilate is beginning to feel he is being drawn into the foreign world of Judaism and is not prepared to consider the profound possibilities of Jesus being a different kind of king, of an unworldly realm.

'Am I a Jew? It is your own people and the chief priests who have handed you over to me: what have you done?'

Pilate takes a step back, it's not his concern as to whether he is king or not, but he needs to know why they accuse him of being one. He is asking Jesus to justify his accusers and thus give him a reason to satisfy their demands.

There is no satisfaction for him in Jesus' reply, only more disturbing words. 'Mine is not a kingdom of this world; if my kingdom were of this world, my own would have fought to prevent my being surrendered to the Jews. But my kingdom is not of this kind.'

Jesus in spite of his appearance has a kingly manner and his air of authority makes Pilate think of him as an equal, there is a bond between the two men, the loneliness of high authority is shared.

'It is you who says that I am a king.' Jesus confronts Pilate with his own words. His encounter with Jesus is again drawing him into another dimension.

Pilate is silent, transfixed as Jesus' raised voice echoes around the chamber. 'Yes I am a king, I was born for this, I came into the world for this: to bear witness to the truth; and all who are on the side of truth listen to my voice.'

For a moment Pilate feels on the edge of eternity. This man has opened his mind to the possibility of a world of different values. His heart is touched by something which he doesn't understand.

His Roman education takes over his thinking, his feelings are suppressed.

Philosophy was his moral guidance, this Jewish spirituality is foreign to him and makes him feel uncomfortable.

Pilate has had enough, this man is beginning to get the better of him. 'Truth, what is that?' he asks. Not waiting for an answer he leaves Jesus and goes to face the noisy crowd outside.

Pilate blurts out before the crowd can voice any more accusations.. 'I find no case against him. But according to a custom of yours I should release one prisoner at the Passover; would you like me then to release the king of the Jews?' Even now he cannot resist some sarcasm.

He has finally surrendered his power to the mob; they now make the decision for him. He has been manipulated by the crowd, he has failed to govern. But this is his last hope. He knows it will be a gross miscarriage of justice if he condemns Jesus without any evidence of guilt.

But the offer doesn't work, they want Barabbas released, not Jesus.

Pilate holds his head in his hands, his thoughts are in turmoil, the Jews brought Jesus before him accused of insurrection without proof, now they want a notorious rebel released, a convicted criminal and a real threat to law and order.

Pilate has finally surrendered all his power to the mob, they can now make the decisions.

50

John 19: 1–11

Pilate then had Jesus taken away and scourged; and after this, the soldiers twisted some thorns into a crown and put it on his head, and dressed him in a purple robe. They kept coming up to him and saying, 'Hail, king of the Jews!' and they slapped him in the face.

Pilate came outside again and said to them, 'Look, I am going to bring him out to you to let you see that I find no case.' Jesus then came out wearing the crown of thorns and the purple robe. Pilate said, 'Here is the man.' When they saw him the chief priests and the guards shouted, 'Crucify him! Crucify him!' Pilate said, 'Take him yourselves and crucify him: I can find no case against him.' 'We have a Law,' the Jews replied, 'and according to that Law he ought to die, because he has claimed to be the Son of God.'

When Pilate heard them say this his fears increased. Re-entering the Praetorium, he said to Jesus, 'Where do you come from?' But Jesus made no answer. Pilate then said to him, 'Are you refusing to speak to me? Surely you know I have power to release you and I have power to crucify you?' 'You would have no power over me,' replied Jesus 'if it had not been given you from above; that is why the one who handed me over to you has the greater guilt.'

❖❖❖

What happened next was related to you by the Roman guard. He told you that after Pilate took Jesus away he had him scourged, a milder form of punishment compared to a Roman flogging from which hardly a man survived.

He told you that Jesus had been stripped to the waist and spread-eagled on a bench. The scourging had been sharp but brief. Pilate's leniency was a result of his uncertainty about the case presented to him.

Because Jesus was only a Jew in the soldiers' eyes they felt free to have some fun with him. They all knew about the talk of him being a king so they cut some twigs off a thorn bush growing in the court yard.

They used Gladiators' gauntlets to twist the thorns into a wreath, then they pressed it onto Jesus' head.

The guard told you how even he felt the pain as the inch long thorns pierced his scalp and forehead, a mesh of needles deep under his skin.

To complete their fun, they put a purple robe on him, repeating Herod's joke with Pilate.

Now he was their king, but a king they could abuse. 'Hail king of the Jews' they would say with mock respect, then slap his face with enough force to draw blood again.

You've heard enough, and now you are with the restless crowd who want to know what Pilate is doing with Jesus inside the Fortress.

Silence falls, Pilate has appeared. 'Where is he?' they all shout.

'Look,' says Pilate, 'I am going to bring him out to you to let you see that I find no case.'

John 19: 1–11

Two guards escort Jesus out in full view of the crowd.

There is a gasp of surprise and laughter as they see Jesus standing dressed in purple and blood streaming down from a crown of thorns on his head.

They can see now what Pilate intended; he finds no case against this man, he is an impotent pretender, humiliation and scourging should be enough punishment.

'Here is the man,' said Pilate, 'not a king, not the son of God, just a man, this surely is enough punishment for him.'

Pilate is stunned when even this fails to satisfy the crowd. The chief priests lead the crowd, with one voice they all shout, 'Crucify him, crucify him.'

Pilate is frightened and exasperated; he screams at the howling crowd. 'Take him yourselves and crucify him; I can find no case against him.' Why you wonder does he say that? He knows they do not have the power to crucify anyone.

Yes they are ready, but unable to crucify him even though their law clearly dictates death to anyone who claims to be the son of God.

Pilate is aware of the threat of insurrection if he doesn't respect their laws.

He is near to panic, he is failing in his role as Governor; he orders the guards to bring Jesus into the Praetorium for him to have a final private interrogation.

'Where do you come from?' he asks. What is Pilate searching for? He already knows he comes from Galilee, what else is there to know? Pilate is clutching at straws; perhaps Jesus will give him just cause to pardon him, or condemn him.

But Jesus is silent and this makes Pilate angry. His frustration increases his sense of failure.

'Are you refusing to speak to me? Surely you know that I have power to release you and I have power to crucify you.'

'You would have no power over me,' replied Jesus, 'if it had not been given to you from above, that is why the one who handed me over to you has the greater guilt.'

In a few words Jesus has lifted an enormous burden of guilt from Pilate's shoulders. The man before him dressed like a fool and close to death is forgiving him for his own weakness and failings. Pilate is just another player in this tragic scene and now feels a kinship with this man, who shows him such compassion.

51

Jesus Is Condemned to Death –

John 19: 12–16

From that moment Pilate was anxious to set him free, but the Jews shouted, 'If you set him free you are no friend of Caesar's; anyone who makes himself king is defying Caesar.' Hearing these words, Pilate had Jesus brought out, and seated himself on the chair of judgement at a place called the Pavement, in Hebrew Gabbatha. It was Passover Preparation Day, about the sixth hour. 'Here is your king,' said Pilate to the Jews. 'Take him away, take him away!' they said. 'Crucify him!' 'Do you want to crucify your king?' said Pilate. The chief priests answered, 'We have no king except Caesar.' So in the end Pilate handed him over to them to be crucified.

❖❖❖

Pilate is still fraught with indecision, wanting to free Jesus, but also fearing an insurrection if he ignores the Jewish law.

Justice and compassion had been roused in Pilate while in the company of Jesus, but when he faces the crowd his courage and integrity fail him.

'If you set him free you are no friend of Caesar's, anyone who makes himself king is defying Caesar.'

Pilate hears again the absurd unfounded accusation.

In exasperation Pilate orders the guards to bring Jesus out for the crowd to see the man they accuse, and then seats himself on the judgement seat. He must use his authority and act as Governor.

'Here is your king,' says Pilate, meaning them to see the helpless figure they accuse.

'Take him away, take him away,' for them the trial is over, they just want him to die. 'Crucify him,' they roar.

Through talking to Jesus, Pilate was beginning to see Jesus as king of a spiritual world and unwisely challenges the crowd, once more using the provocative title.

'Do you want me to crucify your king?'

There is silence; the chief priests step forward and they confront Pilate.

In the silence you look at Jesus standing near Pilate still dressed in purple, the crown of thorns circles his head, his face bruised and bloodied.

Pilate on his seat of power hears the menacing tones of the high priests. 'We have no king except Caesar.'

Pilate cannot bear to look at Jesus who had shown compassion and understanding for him in his anguish.

With his head in his hands and in a broken voice he orders the guard to take Jesus away and prepare him for execution. Pilate knows now that he is beaten, he cannot save Jesus and quickly leaves the court.

52

Jesus Carries His Cross –

John 19: 17-18

They then took charge of Jesus, and carrying his own cross he went out of the city to the place of the skull or, as it was called in Hebrew, Golgotha, where they crucified him with two others, one on either side with Jesus in the middle.

❖❖❖

You are standing now outside the closed gates of the Antonine Fortress. The sun is high in the sky but its rays cannot warm the chillness in your heart.

You have followed Jesus through his hurried trials which have been a mockery of justice.

What you observed during the past night has shocked you and undermined your faith in Roman justice and opened your eyes to the ruthless hatred some of your people have for Jesus.

And now you wait for the final outcome, the cruel execution of a man you know to be innocent of any crime.

You are not alone; many of Jesus' followers wait not knowing what else to do, they just want to be close to this man. They had all received something from him, now they owed him some loyalty.

The large doors open, soldiers move the people aside to make way for the prisoner escort. They appear with Jesus walking between them. Two other prisoners follow with their escorts.

Again you are shocked at Jesus' appearance. His bruised, swollen eyes, the dark stains of dried blood. The wreath of thorns like a crown still pierces his head.

Your fear and dread is increased when you see the ugly awkward cross that now rests on Jesus' shoulder. The base drags behind, its weight makes a deep furrow in the dirt.

Blood already seeps through his clothes from the scourging he received, now the rough wood is reopening the broken skin.

Soldiers clear the way as you follow alongside Jesus through the narrow streets. The people you pass are quiet; some groan, grieving at the sight, others wide-eyed in disbelief. The Jesus they knew could never deserve this.

So you continue to follow; you can hear the heavy rumble of the cross on the paved street. There is a crash and a cry from the crowd,;you see Jesus fallen and on his knees; the cross weighs him down, he hasn't the strength to stand.

The centurion sees that he is too weak to continue; you stand close by and he orders you to take the weight of the cross from Jesus' shoulders.

This moment will remain with you for the rest of your life. At last you can be of service to Jesus in his awful suffering.

You not only lift the cross but you place it on your own shoulder and wait for Jesus to stand up.

Jesus Carries His Cross – John 19: 17–18

The centurion shrugs his armoured shoulders; if this will help him carry out his orders, so be it. He orders the execution party to move onward.

Now you can feel the weight on your back; the splinters of wood sting like bees. Jesus walks beside you, all you can see are his feet. Your heart is full of love, and having him close to you again is great consolation.

You want to look up into his face but you are bent under the cross. You feel his hand on your shoulder, tears fill your eyes, your heart will break.

But you have a job to do, at last you are sharing in his suffering.

You leave the narrow city streets and arrive at the place of execution. You must now put down the cross; the moment has come when you must leave Jesus in the hands of his executioners.

Now you can look into his eyes. There are no words spoken, your eyes tell him of your grief; no longer questioning, you now know this was the only way for him to take and you have helped him do it. He has no regrets or self pity, this is his act of love for his Father and for you.

A soldier pushes you away and orders everyone to descend the hill.

From a distance you see them strip Jesus and lay him spread-eagled on the cross. You see the hammers rise and fall many times and hear the sharp crack of metal as long nails are driven through his hands and feet.

You refuse to take your eyes from this cruel scene and watch, until Jesus is raised, nailed to the cross, which falls with a jolt into the hole prepared for it.

Now there is nothing left for you to do, only wait for him to die.

53

The Crucifixion – Luke 23: 33-46

When they reached the place called The Skull, there they crucified him with two criminals, one on his right, the other on his left. Jesus said, 'Father, forgive them; they do not know what they are doing.' Then they cast lots to share out his clothing.

The people stayed there, watching. As for the leaders, they jeered at him with the words, 'He saved others, let him save himself if he is the Christ of God, the Chosen One.' The soldiers mocked him too, coming up to him, offering him vinegar, and saying, 'If you are the King of the Jews, save yourself.' Above him there was an inscription: 'This is the King of the Jews.'

One of the criminals hanging there abused him: 'Are you not the Christ? Save yourself and us as well.' But the other spoke up and rebuked him. 'Have you no fear of God at all?' he said. 'You got the same sentence as he did, but in our case we deserved it: we are paying for what we did. But this man has done nothing wrong.' Then he said, 'Jesus, remember me when you come into your kingdom.' He answered him, 'In truth I tell you, today you will be with me in paradise.'

It was now about the sixth hour and the sun's light failed, so that darkness came over the whole land until the ninth hour. The veil of the sanctuary was torn right down the middle. Jesus cried out in a loud voice, saying, 'Father, into your hands I commit my spirit.' With these words, he breathed his last.

❖ ❖ ❖

Imagine that you are on the hill outside Jerusalem, not many miles from another hill where the angels had joyfully told the shepherds that a mighty Saviour had been born and would be a source of joy and gladness for the whole world.

But now on this hill, all is darkness.

You are standing on this hill, your head covered against the cold night air.

What sounds can you hear? Soldiers' voices giving orders, the rattle of dice, faint groaning, sudden shouts of pain and anguish coming from above your head.

You hear joking and laughter, and merciless contempt.

You are near the thick wooden cross.

You can't lift your head, you can only look at the base of the cross where it rests deep in the stony ground, thick wooden wedges keeping it secure.

Your eyes are caught by a drop of blood as it splashes on the stones at your feet.

You slowly raise your eyes and look up at the cross before you, and you see the white, bruised, blood-stained body of Jesus hanging there.

He is struggling to breathe; he pushes upwards to allow his chest to expand, the only way he can breathe.

You look at his feet. They are dirty and grazed, fixed to the wood by a huge iron nail driven through both feet and deep into the wood.

The holes grow bigger as he pushes the weight of his body upwards.

You want to touch his feet, the only consolation you can offer. First your fingers touch the hard unforgiving nail, then you feel the stone cold feet.

You look at his legs, the dirt, dried blood, his knees raw and bleeding from falling.

There is dried blood on his body, but there is fresh blood running down the cross from his back, still bleeding after his scourging, and now it rubs against the cross as he tries to breathe.

Your eyes reluctantly look higher and you see the face of Jesus.

What do you see? A grey, bloodless face; his agony makes him groan deep in his chest, beads of sweat sit on his brow and upper lip.

See the dried blood on his face; his eyes are swollen and bruised black from the soldiers' guessing games.

His hair is wet with sweat and blood. Thorns like long needles cover his head; you see how they pierce the skin on his forehead. Blood has run into his eyes and down his neck.

You can hear his back scraping on the wood, every breath an agony; the nails tear at his feet and hands.

Your eyes are on his face. His lips move and you hear him say, 'Father, forgive them. They know not what they do.'

These words bring back the man you knew and loved.

This broken, tortured man had offered you his friendship and told you many heart-warming things, above all that you are loved by his Father and precious in His eyes.

You saw him show great compassion for the mentally and physically ill.

He had given new life to those who had thought of themselves as being beyond redemption.

He had fed the hungry and raised the dead.

Now as you look, the eyes which had always given you encouragement are now closed and you hear him breathe his last breath with the words, 'Father, into your hands I commit my spirit.'

His body becomes limp and still. The full weight of his body hangs from the nails in his hands. He no longer struggles to breathe. The Divine Son is dead.

54

The Burial – Mark 15: 42-47

It was now evening, and since it was Preparation Day (that is, the vigil of the Sabbath), there came Joseph of Arimathaea, a prominent member of the council, who himself lived in the hope of seeing the kingdom of God, and he boldly went to Pilate and asked for the body of Jesus. Pilate, astonished that he should have died so soon, summoned the centurion and enquired if he was already dead. Having been assured of this by the centurion, he granted the corpse to Joseph who brought a shroud, took Jesus down from the cross, wrapped him in the shroud and laid him in a tomb which had been hewn out of the rock. He then rolled a stone against the entrance to the tomb. Mary of Magdala and Mary the mother of Joseph were watching and took note of where he was laid.

❖❖❖

You have followed Jesus from his arrest to his execution. It has taken the Sanhedrin less than twenty-four hours to achieve their relentless desire to destroy Jesus, your beloved master.

You have been standing all day in the hot sun and watched Jesus in agony nailed to the cross. The cross you had carried after he had fallen.

The Burial – Mark 15: 42–47

You had water to drink but he had been offered sour wine.

You have seen the soldiers break the legs of the men crucified either side of Jesus to hasten their death; but this had not been necessary with Jesus; a spear thrust into his side had let out blood and water but there had been no sign of pain.

And now evening has come. Soon it will be the Sabbath; the bodies need to be removed and buried.

You become aware of a man standing near you; it's Joseph, a member of the council which makes up the Sanhedrin.

This man has secretly sympathised with Jesus and had tried to give support to the disciples but never revealed it to the council.

You can see that he is deeply moved and is grieving to see the man he had grown to love and respect die in such a way.

It is too late for him to speak in his defence, but you respond eagerly to his intention to ask Pilate for the body of Jesus, an act which he can perform without offending the vindictive Sanhedrin.

He needs your support and you feel glad to be able to do something to redeem the shameful scene.

You both leave the hill and enter Jerusalem. It's a short walk through the streets to Pilate's residence in the Antonine Fortress.

Waiting in the audience chamber, memories are still fresh in your mind of Pilate wrestling with his desire for justice and his fear of the mob.

He enters the chamber. His mind has been preoccupied with matters during the day which helped him forget his troubled conscience.

Pilate listens to Joseph who is known to be an important member of the council.

When Joseph asks permission to remove the body of Jesus, Pilate looks surprised to learn that he is dead. The speed of the Sanhedrin in effecting the execution has shocked him.

Pilate shows his lack of trust in the Jews and asks the centurion to confirm what Joseph has said.

Yes, it is true, and Pilate is told about the spear being thrust into the body with no sign of pain to be seen.

This satisfies Pilate and he gladly grants Joseph permission to take the body. He hopes this will now be the end of it, and this shameful miscarriage of justice forgotten.

You walk in silence back to the hill and there you begin to remove the body of Jesus from the cross.

Some soldiers remain on guard and help you lift the cross out of its base and place it gently on the ground.

You look down on Jesus, his body drained of blood, still firmly nailed to the cross.

The soldiers have the tools to remove the nails and the efficiency used to hammer them through his flesh is seen again as they free his hands and feet from their grip.

The first thing that you want to do is remove the thorns that still surround his head. You borrow a soldier's knife and cut the thorny wreath into pieces.

It's difficult to remove them; they pierce to the bone and cling like claws with a vicious grip.

With the soldier's drinking water you can now wash Jesus' face. Gently you wipe the dried blood from his brow, his eyes, bruised and swollen, then the cuts on his face made by the soldiers' fists.

The Burial – Mark 15: 42–47

Joseph, more prepared than you thought, produces a shroud. You help to spread it on the ground next to the body still lying on the cross.

Gently you take the head and shoulders while Joseph takes the feet and place the limp body on the shroud.

You take a last look at your master's face.

Then it is covered, and you and Joseph lift the body up into what feels like an embrace. To hold him in your arms fills your heart with grief and love.

Joseph tells you that he has prepared his family tomb, which he offers as a burial place, and slowly you carry Jesus to the rock cliff that borders the cemetery nearby.

You have reached the wall of rock. Here is the black entrance and you carry the body into its darkness.

There in this cave-like tomb is the stone shelf on which the body can rest.

There it will lie undisturbed for twelve months until the bones are collected and placed in the charnel house.

Your last service now completed, you look at the shrouded body, a final farewell.

One last act has to be done. Together you and Joseph roll a heavy stone across the entrance. The rumble of stone echoes deep in the tomb, then silence.

All you hear is the rasping of crickets in the grass as you look up into the night sky. The stars that once rejoiced at his birth are silent now. It's all over. You feel empty and alone – where are the disciples? They must be found.

55

Lectio Divina – Reading with God

– Psalm 130

From the depths I call to you, Yahweh:
Lord, listen to my cry for help.
Listen compassionately
To my pleading.

If You never overlooked our sins, Yahweh,
Lord, could anyone survive?
But You do forgive us,
And for that we revere You.

I wait for Yahweh, my soul waits for Him,
I rely on His promise.
My soul relies on the Lord,
More than a watchman;
On the coming of the dawn.

Let Israel rely on Yahweh
As much as the watchman on the dawn.
For it is with Yahweh that mercy is to be found,
And generous redemption;
It is He who redeems Israel
From all their sins.

❖❖❖

'From the depths I call to You, Yahweh.'

I call from the depths of my soul, I call in my blindness, my uncertainty, my ignorance, from my anxious thoughts I call to You my loving Father.

'Lord, listen to my cry for help.'

My Lord, my Father listen to me, hear me, I place my lips close to Your ear, I speak to You with confidence.

'Listen compassionately to my pleading.'

Hear me, be compassionate, show me Your mercy; as I whisper into Your ear I confide all my thoughts and longings to You, all my regrets.

'If You never overlooked our sins, Yahweh, Lord, could anyone survive?'

I confess my sinfulness, my feelings, my weaknesses, my rejection of your love, my selfishness, conceit, pride. I could not survive if You did not forgive me. I can only tell You because I trust in Your complete forgiveness.

'But You do forgive us, and for that we revere you.'

I can be sure of Your forgiveness, I believe that I am a loved, forgiven sinner and You, Father, have accepted me back into Your family. For this You have my love and profound respect. I can rejoice because I am Your loved son, loved daughter again.

'I wait for Yahweh, my soul waits for Him, I rely on His promise.'

My whole being waits, is waiting, for Your love and forgiveness; my life depends on You, my Father. You made me, I return to You.'

'My soul relies on the Lord.'

I put my complete trust in You, my Father. I turn to You for everything. I can rely on nothing else; I can rely on no one else. There is no one else who can save me.

'More than a watchman on the coming of the dawn.'

As a watchman during a long, cold, dark night longs to see the dawn and feel again the warmth of the sun, so in my darkness I long for You, for Your love, Your forgiveness, Your guidance, Your grace.

'Let Israel rely on Yahweh as much as the watchman on the dawn.'

Let me rely on You, and be as certain of Your love as I am that the sun will dispel the night and create a new day for me.

'For it is with Yahweh that mercy is to be found and generous redemption.'

For it is only with You, my Father, that I can find mercy and forgiveness. No one else can give me peace of mind. Your generosity is beyond my imagining. You can redeem me and give me fullness of life. You can open my eyes, help me understand, and fill me with gladness.

'It is He who redeems Israel from all their sins.'

It is You, my Father; You are the only one who can rescue me. Only You can wash away my sins. It is to You I turn, to You I speak. Only You can save me.

56

The Empty Tomb – John 20: 1–10

It was very early on the first day of the week and still dark when Mary of Magdala came to the tomb. She saw that the stone had been moved away from the tomb and came running to Simon Peter and the other disciple, the one Jesus loved. 'They have taken the Lord out of the tomb,' she said, 'and we don't know where they have put him.'

So Peter set out with the other disciple to go to the tomb. They ran together but the other disciple, running faster than Peter, reached the tomb first; he bent down and saw the linen cloths lying on the ground, but did not go in. Simon Peter who was following now came up, went right into the tomb, saw the linen cloths on the ground, and also the cloth that had been over his head; this was not with the linen cloths but rolled up in a place by itself. Then the other disciple who had reached the tomb first also went in; he saw and he believed. Till this moment they had failed to understand the teaching of scripture, that he must rise from the dead. The disciples then went home again.

❖❖❖

It's early morning. You and Peter are running along the empty streets of Jerusalem. Your mind is in turmoil. For days you have grieved for your beloved master and friend.

The horror of his execution has not diminished and you have sought sad comfort in the wealth of memories that rise unbidden.

Now your wounds have been opened again with Mary's news of the outrage at Jesus' tomb. She has told you that someone has removed the stone and taken his body away. You suspect the Temple authorities; there is no limit to their determination to remove all memory of Jesus.

Now you are racing down the Kidron valley, crossing the stream and then up to the large cemetery on the hill not far from Gethsemane.

Now among the tombs you run, anxious to get to the cliff of rock which holds the body of Jesus, a place you had thought to be safe.

Peter, older than you, is getting breathless; the hill has slowed him down. You cannot wait. Leaving him behind, you keep running until you arrive gasping for breath at the tomb.

What Mary had told you is true; the stone has been moved and the tomb is open.

You bend down to look inside, reluctant to enter, fearing what you might find.

Your eyes grow accustomed to the darkness and gradually bandages can be seen on the floor. Someone has taken Jesus' body from its tomb, and you are paralysed with anger and fear at this outrage.

There are footsteps behind. Peter has caught up with you and is leaning against the wall of the tomb. He has no breath to speak and brushes past to enter the dark tomb.

The Empty Tomb – John 20: 1–10

As usual Peter leads the way and now you follow. Your eyes search the stone chamber. There is the shelf where you had placed the body and which now lies empty. The linen cloths with which you had bound his body lie scattered. Inexplicably the cloth which you had carefully wrapped around his head is neatly folded and lies on the shelf.

Why should anyone remove his burial cloths before they took his body away?

Thoughts come crowding in. You had been present when Jesus had raised Lazarus from his tomb and heard him speak of his own victory over death.

In stunned silence you and Peter leave the tomb. In the sunlight your heart is lifted. Has Jesus conquered death as he said he would?

But where is he to be found?

You are surprised to see Mary standing near. You take her hand and look into her eyes. In them all you can see is grief and fear.

You cannot find the words nor do you have the courage to share with her the incredible thoughts that fill your mind.

You and Peter leave Mary by the tomb. The others must be told and Jesus must be found.

57

Jesus Appears to Mary of Magdala

– John 20: 11–18

Meanwhile Mary stayed outside near the tomb, weeping. Then, still weeping, she stooped to look inside, and saw two angels in white sitting where the body of Jesus had been, one at the head, the other at the feet. They said, 'Woman, why are you weeping?' 'They have taken my Lord away,' she replied, 'and I don't know where they have put him.' As she said this she turned round and saw Jesus standing there, though she did not recognise him. Jesus said, 'Woman, why are you weeping? Who are you looking for?' Supposing him to be the gardener, she said, 'Sir, if you have taken him away, tell me where you have put him, and I will go and remove him.' Jesus said, 'Mary!' She knew him then and said to him in Hebrew, 'Rabbuni!' – which means Master. Jesus said to her, 'Do not cling to me, because I have not yet ascended to the Father. But go and find my brothers, and tell them: I am ascending to my Father and your Father, to my God and your God.' So Mary of Magdala went and told the disciples that she had seen the Lord and that he had said these things to her.

❖❖❖

Jesus Appears to Mary of Magdala – John 20: 11–18

Now in the graveyard all is still and Mary remains standing by the tomb of Jesus alone with her grief. The two disciples have rushed away. They had appeared excited and had spoken of Jesus conquering death, but her desolation forbids any such thoughts.

Her loss is so great and now the theft of his body is an insult too hard to bear.

The man she mourns changed her; he had made her spirit free and brought joy into her life. She cannot face life without him, and can only seek solace in the many memories that fill her heart.

She must look inside the tomb, still unable to believe the awful truth that it is empty with only the burial cloths scattered on the floor.

Inside she feels again the cold dampness. Her eyes filled with tears she looks to where his body has lain.

The tears distort her vision but she can see light coming from where his body should be.

Gradually the light begins to take shape and two human forms appear, one either end of the place where his body had rested.

Mary falls to her knees. The tomb is full of light and then a voice from the light asks, 'Woman, why are you weeping?'

Mary eagerly responds, ready to accept any help; her grief is stronger than any fear, and any help in her great loss she welcomes. Like a child she says, 'They have taken my Lord away and I don't know where they have put him.'

But there is no reply; the light fades and the tomb is in darkness again.

A shadow falls across the floor of the tomb entrance and Mary quickly leaves the tomb, seeking help in finding some explanation for these mysterious happenings.

A man is standing there and asks her, 'Woman, why are you weeping? Who are you looking for?' Mary assumes the stranger to be a gardener and a real source of help in her search.

'Sir, if you have taken him away, tell me where you have put him, and I will go and remove him.'

The stranger says only one word, 'Mary.' The sound of his voice fills her with joy and in the language of her childhood she greets Jesus with great love and respect, 'Rabbuni!' Master.

She falls to her knees, her relief is beyond words and she clings to his clothing, fearing to lose him again.

It is Jesus but he is transformed and his words sound strange in her ears. 'Do not cling to me, because I have not yet ascended to the Father.'

Now he gives her instructions which she is more than willing to obey. 'Go and find the brothers, and tell them: I am ascending to my Father and your Father, to my God and your God.'

Now these are familiar words and Mary is comforted even more on hearing them. It really is Jesus, though changed.

Yes, she knows how important it is to tell the disciples, they must be told. With some reluctance she leaves Jesus and runs after the two disciples. She knows where to find them.

She had entered the graveyard in profound grief; she leaves full of wonder and excitement.

58

The Road to Emmaus –

Luke 24: 13–35

Now that very same day, two of them were on their way to a village called Emmaus, seven miles from Jerusalem, and they were talking together about all that had happened. And it happened that as they were talking together and discussing it, Jesus himself came up and walked by their side, but their eyes were prevented from recognising him. He said to them, 'What are all these things that you are discussing as you walk along?' They stopped, their faces downcast.

Then one of them, called Cleopas, answered him, 'You must be the only person staying in Jerusalem who does not know the things that have been happening there these last few days.' He asked, 'What things?' They answered, 'All about Jesus of Nazareth, who showed himself a prophet powerful in action and speech before God and the whole people, and how our chief priests and our leaders handed him over to be sentenced to death, and had him crucified. Our own hope had been that he would be the one to set Israel free. And this is not all. Two whole days have now gone by since it all happened, and some women from our group have astounded us: they went to the tomb in the early morning, and when they could not find the body, they came back to tell us they had seen a vision of angels who declared he was alive. Some of our friends went to the tomb and found everything exactly as the women had reported, but of him they saw nothing.'

Then he said to them, 'You foolish men! So slow to believe all that the prophets have said! Was it not necessary that the Christ should suffer before entering into His glory?' Then, starting with Moses and going through all the prophets, he explained to them the passages throughout the scriptures that were about himself.

When they drew near to the village to which they were going, he made as if to go on, but they pressed him to stay with them saying, 'It is nearly evening and the day is almost over.' So he went in to stay with them. Now while he was with them at table, he took the bread and said the blessing, then he broke it and handed it to them. And their eyes were opened and they recognised him, but he had vanished from their sight. Then they said to each other, 'Did not our hearts burn within us as he talked to us on the road and explained the scriptures to us?'

They set out that instant and returned to Jerusalem. There they found the eleven assembled together with their companions, who said to them, 'The Lord has indeed risen and appeared to Simon.' Then they told their story of what had happened on the road and how they had recognised him at the breaking of bread.

❖❖❖

It is another hot day, and you and a friend called Cleopas are on your way from Jerusalem to a village called Emmaus. The village is seven miles away; it may take you two or three hours to get there.

The Road to Emmaus – Luke 24: 13–35

As you walk along, your eyes are fixed on the dry stony road beneath your feet; you have no interest in the scenery, the hills or the houses you pass by.

You are both engrossed in conversation. You have a lot to think about and to discuss. Both of you have shared a traumatic experience in Jerusalem.

It's difficult to hold your tongue but you want to hear your companion's view of the awful events, even though you also have a lot to get off your chest.

You are both still in a state of shock and disbelief: only three days ago your close companion and leader had been executed within twelve hours of his arrest.

You are glad to get out of Jerusalem, away from those distressing memories. You still fear the power of the Romans and the hostility of the Temple authorities.

You both keep walking and talking. Feel the stones under your feet, the sun warm on your back.

You become aware of footsteps close behind, and then suddenly there is a man alongside you. You don't pay him much attention; you and your friend don't welcome any interruption.

Why doesn't this stranger overtake you? He has been walking alongside you for some time and he seems to be listening to your conversation.

The stranger speaks and asks, 'What are you discussing as you walk along, my friends?'

You stop dead in your tracks and look at the stranger. He must have heard quite a bit of your conversation and he is only a few miles from Jerusalem, but he is unaware of the events that took place two days ago.

Your companion is incredulous and tells the stranger that he must be the only person who knows nothing about your leader, a great prophet called Jesus, and how the chief priests had handed him over to be crucified. You feel even more saddened by this man's ignorance.

The stranger starts to walk on and you both follow; he is a few paces in front. 'And what's more,' you shout to him, 'women who visited his tomb couldn't find his body; instead they saw angels who said that he is alive again.'

The stranger stops and turns round. His hood hides most of his face, and he shocks you with his reproach, 'You foolish men, slow to believe the full message of the prophets.'

What does he mean? He walks on and you both catch up with him. 'Tell us what you mean,' you say.

The stranger proves to be a learned man. He explains the scriptures beginning with Moses and all the prophecies of Isaiah.

The stranger makes you see that all you had experienced was meant to happen, and you have been part of God's plan. Yes, it all makes sense. You can remember Jesus telling you he was to suffer at the hands of men, in Jerusalem.

You have been so absorbed listening to this man that the miles have disappeared and you have arrived at the village. The stranger says, 'This is where we must part.' You plead with him not to go on; he must come with you: it's nearly evening.

He agrees to come and stay with you.

You are feeling better: this man has lifted your spirits, given you hope and helped you to find some sense in what to you had been a disaster.

Now you are both having supper with the stranger. There, before you on the table, is some bread, wine, meat and fruit. You all enjoy the food and the wine, and even more the company of the stranger. You actually feel like celebrating. You drink more wine.

Such a feeling of peace is so unexpected. A stillness now surrounds the meal table and you reflect on the day's walk.

You see the stranger silently take the bread in his hands. He says a blessing, 'Blessed are You, Father of all creation; we have this bread to eat, fruit of the earth and work of human hands.'

You watch. He gives some bread to your friend and then some to you, placing it in your hands. You eat it. It all feels so right, you close your eyes. You have never felt such peace.

Then, like a flash of lightning, you know this man is Jesus. You open your eyes but he is gone; only an empty seat, a plate with a few crumbs is all that remains.

You and your friend look at each other. Nothing is said; you both know that you have been in the company of Jesus. After several minutes you say quietly, 'We should have known, the way our hearts burned within us as we walked along the road, the only person who ever made us feel like that was Jesus.'

59

Jesus Appears to the Apostles

~ Luke 24: 35-48

Then they told their story of what had happened on the road and how they had recognised him at the breaking of bread. They were still talking about all this when he himself stood among them and said to them, 'Peace be with you!' In a state of alarm and fright, they thought they were seeing a ghost. But he said, 'Why are you so agitated, and why are these doubts stirring in your hearts? See by my hands and my feet that it is I myself. Touch me and see for yourselves; a ghost has no flesh and bones as you can see I have.' And as he said this he showed them his hands and his feet. Their joy was so great that they still could not believe it, as they were dumbfounded, so he said to them, 'Have you anything here to eat?' And they offered him a piece of grilled fish, which he took and ate before their eyes.

Then he told them, 'This is what I meant when I said, while I was still with you, that everything written about me in the Law of Moses, in the prophecies and in the psalms, was destined to be fulfilled.' He then opened their minds to understand the scriptures, and he said to them, 'So it is written that the Christ would suffer and on the third day rise from the dead, and that, in his name, repentance for the forgiveness of sins would be preached to all nations, beginning from Jerusalem. You are witness to this.'

Jesus Appears to the Apostles – Luke 24: 35–48

❖ ❖ ❖

Imagine that you have been one of the disciples on the road to Emmaus. You and your friend Cleopas have returned from Emmaus to Jerusalem as quickly as you could. You had encountered Jesus during a meal when he had broken the bread.

You are very excited on your walk back to Jerusalem; your legs couldn't move fast enough; you couldn't wait to tell the others.

When you had left Jerusalem, your talk had been full of sadness and despair. Now your joy and gladness give wings to your feet and you race back to Jerusalem.

No one had believed the women who had found the empty tomb and reported that two angels had told them Jesus had risen from the dead. Peter also had found the tomb empty except for the binding cloths.

Now you know why they didn't find Jesus' body: he is alive; he has conquered death, as he promised. This journey, bearing such great news, is the happiest experience of your life, and you can't wait to see the disciples' faces when you tell them.

You know where to find them; they will still be hiding in the upper room, the last place you had seen Jesus before Gethsemane. You arrive.

You rush up the stairs and enter the upper room, the room that holds so many memories for all of you.

You throw open the door and shout a greeting.

Depressed faces look up, surprised to see your excited happy face and hear your joyful greeting.

You sit down at the long table where Jesus had celebrated the Passover meal, and you share with them the wonderful news. Not only had Jesus appeared to you in the breaking of the bread, but he had explained to you how all that had happened to him was part of God's plan which had started with Moses and the prophets.

All is well, no need for anyone to despair. Jesus has overcome death and is risen from the dead.

As you speak, you see the incredulous expressions on the disciples' faces suddenly change to alarm; they no longer look at you, but intently stare over your shoulder at something behind you.

They begin to move away from you – what is wrong with them? What have you said?

You turn around to see what they could be looking at. And there stands the same person you met on the road to Emmaus.

You recognise him immediately, but the others think that they are looking at a ghost.

The ghost speaks; in his familiar, clear voice Jesus says, 'Peace be with you.'

He asks, 'Why are you so frightened? And why all this talk of loss and despair?'

The disciples are silent. They still keep their distance from Jesus; some are moving towards the door.

You want to reassure them and tell them this is Jesus; he has appeared again as he did on the Emmaus road.

But you are silent. Jesus will deal with the situation in his own way.

Jesus Appears to the Apostles – Luke 24: 35–48

Jesus takes a step nearer to the disciples and invites them to look closely at his hands and feet. 'Yes, see the wounds,' he says. 'It really is me, nothing else.'

He moves closer. Fear has left the disciples; now incredible wonder lights up their faces.

To finally convince them that he is not a ghost, he holds out his hands and invites them to hold them. You watch as all the disciples in turn grasp Jesus' hands, not so much to gain proof that he really is flesh and blood but with gladness they welcome him into their company again.

You don't need any more proof but you take his hand in love and respect. You feel the warmth of his hand, still carpenter's hands but now open wounds show his integrity.

The disciples don't doubt that Jesus is with them but they are still unable to take it all in. They are dumbfounded and just sit looking at him in speechless wonder.

Then, true to his nature, he breaks the spell and reminds them they are lacking in hospitality. 'Have you anything to eat?' he asks.

All, yourself included, spring into action. There is great confusion as everyone rushes to get the grilled fish, freshly caught and prepared for this evening.

You crowd around Jesus at the table and watch him eat the fish.

And while you sit down he tells you all again what you heard on the road to Emmaus.

But he goes further. The disciples can understand all he said about the fulfilment of the prophecies and all that had been written about him in the Law of Moses, but as they listen they sense that their minds are clearing; they can think logically, realistically and discern the truth more easily. Their minds are opened; they have eyes to see and ears to hear, ready to receive the Grace of God.

And the true purpose of his suffering and resurrection is that through his name, anyone who asks for forgiveness will become reconciled with God.

'You,' he says, 'are witnesses to everything you have seen and heard; all that is necessary to enable you to spread the good news, that everyone is loved and forgiven.'

You have shared his death, now you can share in establishing his kingdom.

60

Jesus at the Lakeside –

John 21: 1–17

Later on, Jesus revealed himself again to the disciples. It was by the Sea of Tiberias, and it happened like this: Simon Peter, Thomas (called the Twin), Nathanael from Cana in Galilee, the sons of Zebedee and two more of his disciples were together. Simon Peter said, 'I'm going fishing.' They replied, 'We'll come with you.' They went out and got into the boat but caught nothing that night.

When it was already light, there stood Jesus on the shore, though the disciples did not realise that it was Jesus. Jesus called out, 'Haven't you caught anything, friends?' And when they answered, 'No,' he said, 'throw the net out to starboard and you'll find something.' So they threw the net out and could not haul it in because of the quantity of fish. The disciple whom Jesus loved said to Peter, 'It is the Lord.' At these words, 'It is the Lord,' Simon Peter tied his outer garment round him (for he had nothing on) and jumped into the water. The other disciples came on in the boat, towing the net with the fish; they were only about a hundred yards from land.

As soon as they came ashore they saw that there was some bread there and a charcoal fire with fish cooking in it. Jesus said, 'Bring some of the fish you have just caught.' Simon Peter went aboard and dragged the net ashore, full of big fish, one hundred and fifty-three of them, and, in spite of there being so many, the net was not broken. Jesus said to them, 'Come and have breakfast.' None of the disciples were bold enough to ask, 'Who are you?' They knew quite well it was Jesus. Jesus then stepped forward, took the bread and gave it to them, and the same with the fish. This was the third time that Jesus revealed himself to the disciples after rising from the dead.

When they had eaten, Jesus said to Simon Peter, 'Simon, son of John, do you love me more than these others do?' He answered, 'Yes, Lord, you know I love you.' Jesus said to him, 'Feed my lambs.' A second time he said to him, 'Simon, son of John, do you love me?' He replied, 'Yes, Lord, you know I love you.' Jesus said to him, 'Look after my sheep.' Then he said to him a third time, 'Simon, son of John, do you love me?' Peter was hurt that he asked him a third time, 'Do you love me?' and said, 'Lord, you know everything; you know I love you.' Jesus said to him, 'Feed my sheep.'

❖ ❖ ❖

Imagine you are one of the disciples. Jesus has appeared to you all several times since his death.

Now you are without him again, his presence is not with you, and you miss him terribly.

All day you have languished together by the lake. It was here you first met Jesus. It was on this shore that he called you, you followed him, your life changed completely.

Now you are trying to pick up the pieces of your life.

You can't go back to your old life as a fisherman. Your heart is not in it. All day you have fished and caught nothing.

Evening has come, and the day has been fruitless.

Peter, in his usual impatient way, stands up; he must do something.

He says he must try and fish once more, perhaps tonight lamps will attract the fish.

You feel glad someone has taken the initiative and gladly stand up and follow Peter.

You walk across the sandy shore, just a few yards wide, and reach the water's edge. You then get into the old familiar boat.

Hear the water lapping against the sides.

Feel the hard seat beneath you, your feet on the wooden boards.

You place your oar into the rowlock; hear it rattle.

Peter takes the rudder and gives the order to start rowing.

You are glad to be doing something; it takes your mind off the sad thoughts, the empty, lost feeling of nowhere to go, the lack of purpose.

You are now in the middle of the lake, the black sky above, filled with stars. Your eyes wander over them; their brightness never fails to impress you. Where is Jesus? Is he among them?

Why has he left you again? The wind has gone out of your sails, your life is in the doldrums.

Time to draw in the nets; feel the rough, wet net as you haul it on-board.

It's empty! Not one fish.

When will this depression end?

Peter is angry; all night you have fished and have nothing to show.

You look at the hills on the eastern side of the lake.

The sun has begun to rise, like gold footlights on a blue velvet curtain.

Peter decides to return to shore and you begin to row.

The air is still, silent; no one speaks. Hear the splashing, the creaking of the oars.

You are now near the shore. Colour has returned to the lake; the sun is up; a light mist hangs over the water. See the pale blue, calm surface of the lake.

On the shore stands the figure of a man, next to your landing point, but you think nothing of it; you have no fish to sell.

The man on the shore is speaking to you; his voice is clear and rings like a bell in the still morning air.

'Have you caught any fish?' he asks.

Your heart suddenly quickens; the voice, the words are all very familiar and remind you of the first time you met Jesus.

'No, nothing,' you reply.

Now you and all the disciples are wide awake and look keenly at the man on the shore.

'Throw your net on the right side of the boat and you will catch some.'

The voice makes you obey without question.

Hear the splash as you throw the net into the water.

Jesus at the Lakeside – John 21: 1–17

When you haul it alongside you are amazed and delighted: it's full of fish, their tails thrashing, flashing silver.

It's too heavy to pull on-board. Then, in a quiet voice John, without taking his eyes off Jesus, says to Peter, 'It is the Lord.'

You know he is right. Gladness fills you, a feeling you thought you had lost forever,

Peter explodes into action and hastily puts on his garment, jumps out of the boat and walks in the shallow water towards his beloved master.

You and the others row as fast as you can to follow Peter to the shore.

Take your oar out of its rowlock and put it on the bottom of the boat.

You climb over the boat's side and get into the water; it's up to your knees. Feel the soft sand under your feet.

You go up to Jesus. You feel alive again: to see him, to hear his voice has changed everything.

You notice Jesus is as considerate as ever: he has made a small fire and is cooking fish for your breakfast and some bread from the village.

You sit by the fire with Jesus, eating the food he has cooked for you. You feel complete again, you feel reborn.

Jesus is next to you. He looks into your face; see his face, his eyes as they look into yours. He speaks your name; hear him say it. Jesus asks, 'Do you love me?'

What is your answer?

61

Pentecost – Acts 2: 1–13

When Pentecost day came round, they had all met together, when suddenly there came from heaven a sound as of a violent wind which filled the entire house in which they were sitting; and there appeared to them tongues as of fire which separated and came to rest on the head of each of them. They were all filled with the Holy Spirit and began to speak different languages as the Spirit gave them power to express themselves.

Now there were devout men living in Jerusalem from every nation under heaven, and at this sound they all assembled, and each one was bewildered to hear these men speaking his own language. They were amazed and astonished. 'Surely,' they said, 'all these men speaking are Galileans? How does it happen that each of us hears them in his own native language? Parthians, Medes and Elamites; people from Mesopotamia, Judea and Cappadocia, Pontus and Asia, Phrygia and Pamphylia, Egypt and the parts of Libya round Cyrene; residents of Rome – Jews and proselytes alike – Cretans and Arabs: we hear them preaching in our own language about the marvels of God. Everyone was amazed and perplexed; they asked one another what it all meant. Some, however, laughed it off. 'They have been drinking too much new wine,' they said.

❖ ❖ ❖

Imagine that you are one of the disciples, and you are in the familiar upper room celebrating the feast of Pentecost, the Jewish Harvest Festival. Look around the room.

Over the last seven weeks since Jesus' crucifixion you and your friends have been through experiences which have astounded and frightened you.

Since Jesus' death, women have reported seeing him alive and his tomb empty, but no one believed them.

Then Cleopas had told everyone of his experiences on the road to Emmaus.

You were still full of doubt until you saw Jesus for yourself on the shores of Lake Tibereas and in this very upper room. It was then that he had instructed you to stay in Jerusalem until you were given power from God and baptised with the Holy Spirit. He had spoken before of sending His Spirit to be your advocate, and this advocate would stand by you, be on your side to help and guide you.

He wanted you to be a witness and tell Jerusalem all you knew about him, and not just Jerusalem, but the whole world.

But, here you are, still hiding, protecting each other from the Temple authorities, still no courage to speak about all the things you had experienced.

Who would or could believe you? All your memories, so many, joyful, some frightening, challenging – where would you start?

Now in this room, the talk is endless about the significance of the Passover meal. It was beginning to make sense; Jesus had been present again in the breaking of the bread.

What would happen tonight when the bread was broken?

The crushing fear still remains with you from the night Jesus was arrested and taken away to be executed; still you are haunted with shame because you deserted him after all your promises.

Rashly, you had said that you would die with him, but you had disowned him and ran away to hide from his enemies.

These enemies are still present, powerful authorities belonging to the Temple; they had used the Romans to destroy Jesus and all your hopes and expectations.

You have been wonderfully consoled by the presence of Jesus in this room, but he has left you again, and the old fears quickly return that make you dread the future.

You don't really know what is expected of you. Yes, he had said that you were to be a witness to Jerusalem and beyond.

But what would be the consequences? What would you be getting into? It would surely reawaken the hostility of the Temple authorities. They had shown their cunning and ruthless hatred of Jesus; you had escaped from their fury; you don't want to incur their anger again.

In spite of knowing for certain that Jesus had conquered death, you still live in a dangerous world; you have no more courage now than on that awful night when you ran away to hide.

So now the feast of Pentecost, the Harvest thanksgiving, must be observed. The fruits of the earth and work of men's hands now mean more to you. The bread and wine at this meal evoke the presence of Jesus.

Picture the upper room. You sit at a long table, people on benches either side, but Jesus' place is empty.

See the plates, the knives, bread, fruit, wine in your cup before you. Candles light the room, on the tables and the wall.

Pentecost – Acts 2: 1–13

All the disciples are eating and drinking.

There is not much talking, no confident ideas as to what should be done from here on.

You still feel abandoned, lost without your leader.

You have nothing to say, you are silent, thinking about the future, afraid and uncertain.

There is a depression in the room, the air is thick and heavy, thoughts are woolly, no sense of purpose.

Your gaze wanders away from the table and the people near you; you look through the window into the night.

See the bright stars, shining like diamonds in the clear black sky, see them as they sparkle and shimmer.

You suddenly feel a cold draught; fresh air is filling the room. The stuffy atmosphere has gone; your head is clear as if you have just woken up.

The draught now turns into a strong rushing wind – where is it coming from? All the candles go out, the room is in darkness; still the wind fills the room; the whole house is filled with energy. You instinctively hold onto the tablecloth and your cup of wine.

People are crying out, 'What's happening?' But no one moves.

The mighty wind stops as suddenly as it started; the room is still and silent and in darkness.

At first you think you see the stars falling from the sky and entering the room through the roof.

In the silence people look up and their faces are lit, not with stars but with tongues of flame that quietly come to rest on each person's head.

You also feel the warmth of this gentle flame as it rests on your head; it lights up your face and fills your whole body with gladness.

It feels like the presence of Jesus, but he feels closer now than ever. The Spirit, the Advocate has arrived as he had promised.

You at last feel energised, confident. It is clear now. This was all predicted by Jesus. What you do from now on is all part of God's plan.

You will be a witness; you had been with Jesus from the start. You have survived the good times and the bad. You have a lot to tell; things are making sense; there is no need to be afraid of the truth.

Jesus' integrity is perfect, the world must know.

The Spirit of God has become part of you and, no matter what happens, all will be well.

The room is now filled with excited voices; a sense of relief and purpose has energised everyone.

You want to get out, feel free, hide no more, stand on your own two feet and tell the world the truth.

The people outside attracted by the lights are laughing at you.

They say you have been drinking too much wine.

You laugh with them; nothing can spoil your peace, your gladness and immense gratitude. Because Jesus is now part of you and you are part of him and nothing can separate you again. He will never leave you again. Jesus has given you his blessing; he can never take it back.

Paul's Prayer (Ephesians 3: 14–21)

This, then, is what I pray, kneeling before the Father from whom every family, whether spiritual or natural, takes its name. Out of His infinite glory, may He give you the power through His Spirit for your hidden self to grow strong, so that Christ may live in your hearts through faith, and then, planted in love and built on love, you will with all the saints have strength to grasp the breadth and the length, the height and the depth, until, knowing the love of Christ, which is beyond all knowledge, you are filled with the utter fullness of God.

Glory be to Him whose power, working in us, can do infinitely more than we can ask or imagine. Glory be to Him from generation to generation in the Church and in Christ Jesus for ever and ever. Amen.

62

Lectio Divina – Reading with God – John 14: 23–27

Jesus replied, 'Anyone who loves me will keep my word, and my Father will love him, and we shall come to him and make a home in him. Anyone who does not love me does not keep my word. And the word that you hear is not my own: it is the word of the Father who sent me. I have said these things to you while still with you; but the Paraclete, the Holy Spirit, whom the Father will send in my name, will teach you everything and remind you of all I have said to you. Peace I bequeath to you, my own peace I give you, a peace which the world cannot give, this is my gift to you. Do not let your hearts be troubled or afraid.'

❖ ❖ ❖

'If anyone loves me he will keep my word.

'You have experienced your Father's love through being my disciples. You have learned many things; you slowly came to understand that God's love doesn't come from the world but is found within you and among you.

'I have taught you to love God as your Father and to love Him with all your heart, with all your mind and with all your strength, and also to love one another.

'If anyone loves me he will keep my word, and my Father will love him.

'If you do as I say you will always be in God's love.

'And we shall come to him and make our home with him.

'I and my Father will come to you and make our home in you. We will be closer to you than the marrow in your bones. You will be our home, our temple and you can feel at home with us. You need to hide nothing from us. Whatever you may be doing, or feeling or thinking, we will still be with you.

'Those who do not love me do not keep my word.

'Because you were happy being with me, you felt safe and loved and learned of things you could never have imagined, you will want to do all I ask of you. You will be changed through knowing and loving me.

'And my word is not my own, it is the word of the one who sent me.

'The things you have heard me say, the things you saw me do, the love and the freedom you experienced through being with me were only possible because they were what your Father wanted.

'I have said these things to you while still with you, but the advocate, the Holy Spirit, who the Father will send in my name, will teach you everything and remind you of all I have said to you.

'You remember how you learned about the scriptures about the new kingdom, how your eyes and ears were opened to the truth; you found a new freedom and life-giving spirit. I was the teacher you loved; you felt safe with me. But I cannot be physically with you forever; your Father will send the life-giving spirit to be at home with you forever.

'This living spirit will be in my name; he will teach you and guide you as I did. He will always be on your side; he will lead you on your journey to the Father. He will be your advocate and present you favourably before God. All your faults and shortcomings will be overlooked and forgiven and you will be accepted by your Father at all times.

'This Holy Spirit will be your counsellor; turn to him in your prayers and he will guide you on your path home to the Father.

'The Holy Spirit I have won for you will protect you from harm, protect you from taking the wrong path. He will show you the right way, show you the truth and give you life in abundance.

'Peace I bequeath to you, my own peace I give you, a peace the world cannot give: this is my gift to you.

'True peace of mind and harmony with God, your creator, is what I leave you. This is my peace: profound, indestructible peace I give you. The world can give many pleasures, is a beautiful and wonderful place created by the Father, but you were made for a greater happiness which only God can give you, a greater peace and fulfilment which only I can give you.

'Do not let your hearts be troubled or afraid.

'Try and control your anxieties, trust in me, turn to God and rely on the Holy Spirit to guide you through the storm.

'The love of the Father is greater than life itself. You have His love: the Holy Spirit will guide you and support you through the good times and the bad times on your path home. Your Father wants you back in His family.'

63

Three-way Conversation

The disciples had often watched Jesus as he prayed. They also had prayed all their lives, in the synagogue or the Temple.

But Jesus' way of praying must have seemed different.

'Show us how to pray,' they asked him; his way must have seemed better.

Jesus directs them to speak to Yahweh to whom they had always prayed, but now they are invited to think of Him in a different way, and to address Him in a most intimate manner, different from what they had been taught all their lives.

We also are invited by Jesus to call God not only Father but 'Dad', to make us feel that we are the children of a loving, understanding Father.

To be able to reach that intimate relationship with God, St Ignatius has left us a method of prayer which might enable us to pray more confidently, more intimately with God.

So, now remembering those words of Cardinal Newman, 'Imagination is the high road of faith,' we enter this Ignatian way of praying together.

In your mind's eye, firstly picture Mary, the Virgin Mother of God.

What is your favourite image of Mary; is she young or more mature?

She carried the Son of God in her womb.

She had been his world, as all our mothers were to us as children.

She had been the greatest influence in the formation of Jesus' character as he moved from boyhood into manhood.

She had suffered as no one else could during his trial and crucifixion.

And now she is before you, it was Jesus' wish that she should be your spiritual mother also.

Her smiling face encourages you to speak.

What would you like to say to her? What are your worries at the moment? Share them with her; tell her your heartfelt wishes and needs.

Now you have a special request; you ask her to take you to her Son, Jesus. Mary comes and stands beside you.

Perhaps you let her take your hand. She leads you forward, and there before you is Jesus, her Son. You hear Mary tell Jesus your name, and that you want to speak to him.

What is your image of Jesus as he stands before you?

Still holding Mary's hand, you look into Jesus' face, and repeat all that you shared with Mary.

And now with Mary's support, you ask Jesus to show you his Father, your Father also, the Father he also wants you to address.

Jesus now reaches out and you let him take your other hand. With Mary one side and Jesus the other, they lead you into God's presence.

What is your favourite image of the Father? A face pleased to see you; He knows; He understands.

Speak to Him also from the heart and tell Him everything that concerns you at the moment. With Mary and Jesus at your side, you can tell Him anything or just stand in His presence.

64

Isaiah 55: 1–3

Oh, come to the water all you who are thirsty;
though you have no money come!
Buy corn without money, and eat,
and, at no cost, wine and milk.
Why spend money on what is not bread,
your wages on what fails to satisfy?
Listen, listen to me, and you will have good
things to eat and rich food to enjoy.
Pay attention, come to me;
listen, and your soul will live.

❖ ❖ ❖

'Oh, come to the water all you who are thirsty; though you have no money come!'

What is your heart's desire, your deepest longing? From childhood you needed to be loved, to be able to love, to feel secure, to feel valued. You don't need money to receive your hidden longings. Come to me your Creator and I will give them to you in abundance beyond your imagining. Just ask and you will receive.

> *'Buy corn without money, and eat, and, at no cost, wine and milk.'*

Like the food and drink you need to live, so the nourishment you need for your spirit can be bought without money. Where could such a market place be found?

> *'Why spend money on what is not bread, your wages on what fails to satisfy?'*

Why would you spend money on what fails to nourish your body or waste your lives pursuing what does not fulfil your spirit's longing?

> *'Listen, listen to me, and you will have good things to eat and rich food to enjoy.'*

Have the ears of the disciple and listen to my words, and you will receive rich nourishment for your body and spirit.

> *'Pay attention, come to me, listen, and your soul will live.'*

Give me your full attention, some of your time, use your intelligence and listen to the one that loves you. You will never know me unless you look for me; I can be found in your deepest longings, I can fulfil them and in that freedom you can become the person you were born to be.

65

Isaiah 55: 6–9

*Seek Yahweh while he is still to be found,
call him while he is still near.
Let the wicked man abandon his way,
the evil man his thoughts.
Let him turn back to Yahweh who will take
pity on him to our God who is rich in forgiving;
For my thoughts are not your thoughts,
my ways not your ways - it is Yahweh who speaks.
Yes the heavens are as high above the earth
as my ways, my thoughts above your thoughts.*

❖❖❖

'Seek Yahweh while he is still to be found, call him while he is still near.'

Search your heart, look for God, now is your chance, life is short, call on Him now, He is nearer to you than the marrow in your bones or the air that you breathe. He awaits your attention and longs to hear your voice.

'Let the wicked man abandon his way, the evil man his thoughts.'

Are you a prisoner involved with that which only brings anguish and disappointment? Anything that distresses you can be shared with me.

'Let him turn back to Yahweh who will take pity on him, to our God who is rich in forgiving.'

Your back may be turned to God, but whenever you decide to turn and face Him He will understand and forgive you, his beloved son, beloved daughter. He is rich in mercy and his generosity is beyond your imaginings.

'For my thoughts are not your thoughts, my ways not your ways - it is Yahweh who speaks.'

You have your thoughts and illusions, your judgements and opinions, perceptions and conclusions, likes and dislikes and they are yours not mine. I am Yahweh your Father and my thoughts are different from yours. I am the truth and it is difficult for you to see me.

'Yes the heavens are as high above the earth as my ways, my thoughts above your thoughts.'

Yes we are different, as different as the sky is from the earth, your thoughts and my thoughts are incompatible. Reach out to me and I will share my thoughts with you, you will see the truth and be free.

66

The Sign of the Cross, Stilling

Imagine making the sign of the cross on your forehead and saying, 'In the name of the beloved Father.'

Your head, the seat of your understanding, your memory, your inspiration. The originator of all your thoughts, containing all your knowledge.

It could represent God, the source of all wisdom, all imaginings, all ideas and desires.

The beloved father enlightens your mind in prayer and broadens your comprehension.

Now imagine making the sign of the cross over your mouth and saying, 'In the name of the beloved Son.'

As Jesus was the mouthpiece of God and gave expression to his Father's message, so are our words an expression of love for the Father and of His love for our brothers and sisters.

Our words are again an incarnation of the Logos. Jesus lives again in the words we speak.

The Logos has been made flesh for eternity.

And now imagine slowly making the sign of the cross over your heart and saying, 'In the name of the beloved Holy Spirit.'

Your heart, the source of your love and compassion. The temple of the Holy Spirit.

The Holy Spirit promised to us by Jesus, who won this great gift for us through his passion.

It lives forever in our hearts, helping us to pray, turning our hearts of stone to flesh, making us truly human, enabling us to love the Father and our neighbour.

'The beloved Father, the beloved Son, the beloved Holy Spirit.' We have the Holy Trinity within us, truly gifted and saved.

We thank you Lord for the wonder of our being and the miracle of your presence in me and every person.